NON-CAPITAL WEALTH
Ajani Abdul-Khaliq

Social Arts
2020

First Printing: 2020

ISBN: 978-1-7337455-7-4

Social Arts & Technical Alliance
https://thesata.com

Ordering Information:
Special discounts are available on quantity purchases by corporations, associations, educators, and others. For details, contact the publisher at the above listed address.

Table of Contents

Table of Contents

Table of Contents

Chapter 1: Introduction

Many of us have been conditioned to worry about money—to build our lives around its acquisition, to limit our relationships based on others' ability to provide it. No matter how much we have or don't have, we modern Westerners are encouraged to keep a ready place at our psychological table for money and its importance—where even the very rich are sometimes inclined to live trapped lives, ironically held captive by the objects and social circles that bear status. We expect to make even more money and obligate ourselves to buy newer, even richer things even if that nice old dresser from Goodwill might suit us better.

But there is an odd quality associated with money that we all surely know about: Because its flow from giver to receiver is where a large part of the excitement lies—because having had a lot of it once upon a time probably does you no good now—money truly is an ethereal sort of thing. It's there but it isn't. It buys necessities and luxuries alike, but does not buy our long-term contentment with the items we've bought. We're told that money makes the world go round, but we also know that our satisfaction with that world largely lies in the hands of people and the behaviors they display. Some of us go round and round in a happy world; many of us simply send more money whirling into an unhappy one. The importance given to money is so great that we even frame essential phenomena like risk, education, and time in terms of it even though these and other life experiences should be (and overwhelmingly are) free by nature.

Perhaps the weight we give to money can be explained by its basic economic definition. Money is

- **a store of value**: we use it to quickly assess the worth of any object or service we wish to trade; that house, those 10 cars, three college educations, and eight years of median-paid work are worth approximately the same amount.

- **a unit of account**: we use it to keep track of how much of that stored value has been built up over time in a certain place; a certain person's bank account might have 15 years' worth of work minus 18 years of family and leisure stored in it.

- **a medium of exchange**: we use it to translate the giver's assignment of worth into the language of the receiver; thanks to money, my paintings become food for your kids.

In this way money, like sound or electricity, can be thought of as the "energy carrier" for publicly agreed-upon value. In fact, money is an even better energy carrier than sound, electricity, or even its celebrated partner—time—because the ways in which each individual uses these three varies greatly depending on how their lives are set up. No wonder we give so much importance to the green. Among societies full of strangers whose values are not easily translated, a moneyless trading system is a lot like an electrical system with no wires. Yes it's definitely possible, but the work we'll need to put in for directing our aims will require a lot more advancement in how we understand those aims—in ourselves and in the people we're trading with.

Barring that understanding, money can and should remain the preferred vehicle for transporting abstract value among people and groups...

But now we have a problem.

One of the fundamental principles of economics is that the resources we use are scarce. Almost anything we use in the practical world has a finite limit placed on it, so that most things will eventually run out if overused. This is as true for human time expenditure and "good" job opportunities as it is for forests and gold mines. Eventually the pool of what we want dries up—or at least that's what traditional Western economic theory claims.

Among other implications, the scarcity of economic objects means there will eventually be a limit on the number of sufficiently-paying jobs that fit within the average person's ability to perform (for if the average person could do it, such jobs could be expected to pay less). On the other hand, we can also expect there to be a very high number of people *and companies* who want to be rich. As society progresses and the opportunities for innovation grow, the number of avenues for those who want to become rich also increases. But this typically requires that those people had above average, non-normal access to the tools, money, knowledge, and networks for innovation in the first place. So the rich really do get richer—though such riches aren't always monetary. They also become more numerous. Building on compounded expertise, more of such groups are also likely to merge. In a governing state where these same rich systems are more likely to have access to political power, we might not be surprised to find relaxed regulatory limits on these systems' ability to grow larger, so that Google for example does not have to face the same kinds of antitrust action that Microsoft faced years before. And what does this mean for the (monetarily) average person?

> More and bigger groups—more complex webs of banking, insurance, communications, media and entertainment, largely tech-based—place a claim on the value we bring into the home.

Even though many of our favorite service providers are benign enough, their good and often socially responsible leanings won't reduce the number of them which we are increasingly required to deal with. The number of rich are growing, but the number of people and families who are monetarily dependent on those rich are growing faster. Meanwhile, the growing complexity of spaces occupied by the rich has also made the power structures to which they have access more complex. So the tech culture, oil culture, banking culture, insurance culture, the medical field, the entertainment industry, and the retirement industry for example, each have each other to contend with. From there, the rich in money become poorer in political mobility <u>relative to their tier</u> UNLESS they gain the favor of the non-rich in money to back them. Thus (monetarily speaking)

> under general population growth, the number of non-rich increase as the number of rich increase to extract value from them, with the wealth of the former increasing faster than that of the latter.

This is a conjecture on the basic definition of a widening wealth gap. In remaining close to its consumers, even the modern mega-company knows that it must adopt a certain branding or subscription path, or otherwise lose to its sworn competitor. It turns out that being rich isn't necessarily what the non-rich think it is. What good are five porsches when your personal agenda is forever bound to the status conferred by those around you?

Karl Marx would have said that the rich building their fortunes upon the backs of the non-rich would lead to an uprising among the non-rich once they grew tired of being exploited. So he and his associates advocated a communist society in which individuals' ability to acquire riches would be checked by the equalizing power of a classless society. But that hasn't really happened anywhere in earnest, save for small groups of enthusiasts like Mao, Lenin, and Castro conducting uprisings on their own WITHOUT the aid of the rest of the majority non-rich they claimed to represent. To the extent that the non-rich don't actually *feel* they're being exploited, there's no need to war with their landlords. Because the *non-rich* have a certain set of privileges that the rich don't have:

> As the rich become so at the monetary expense of the non-rich, they become stuck to the systems that draw such expense. The non-rich become accustomed to a certain stability in the systems on which they have become dependent, and where capitalism is allowed to prevail, the same competition that helped the rich rise is also the system that keeps the rich competing against at least one eternal (also rich) opponent.

The possibility of moving from one "exploiter" to another means that the non-rich enjoy a level of choice that their monetary masters cannot indulge. A slave with the freedom to travel between two masters may be freer than the masters themselves—each dependent on that slave's continued provision of value.

And so we have a natural tendency toward the two-group "niche" monopoly: Fox vs CNN, AFC vs NFC, Democrats vs Republicans, Mac vs PC, Uber vs—in the absence of legal support for alternatives, for example—the regulators. If you are a mega company and you should ever succeed in crushing your sworn enemy, the consumer's need for a choice between a [personally validating brand] and an [interpersonally enabling brand] means that on some days he will enjoy the convenience you provide him, other days he will want you to sponsor the work he wishes to express himself: the socially connective versus the individually elaborating. The chances are low that any single business can do both. And if it tries, at least one of those types of consumer will become angry with him—earning a true (even if only legalistic) uprising for the perceived lack of options. So no, it's not likely that any one version of anything will ever take over our worlds *completely*. Christianity and Islam, Mother and Father, the inwardly validating and the outwardly expressive demand each other's company, so that we as consumers can expect to have our pick—whether we're rich or not.

Now if there's always a second choice, what's our alternative to money-centered capitalism itself?

The point of the above discussion was for us to get a general feel for the consumer terrain we live in. Maybe there really are more places digging into our pockets than our bank accounts can handle. But money isn't the only measure of value. The systems that pull money from us also partner with their competitors to give us freedom of choice in exchange. The irony of all this is that, even if we were to gain all the money we wanted, we would likely use that money to buy—guess what—more freedom of choice. We might buy that yacht, but not necessarily because we knew anything about boats or even liked sailing. We might buy that house in the Glades of Bourbonshire, but not because it was the only place we could stand living— maybe because it *looked* the part when all we really wanted was quiet and security. Some of us indeed get richer, but as we do so the space of choices becomes *narrower* in the social sense, not wider. That is, even though we "could" purchase more things in theory, we're discouraged from considering lower-tier versions of those things in actuality. We stop considering RVs and apartment complexes and look among the mansions only. Even though the former might be wicked fun while the latter might simply be greener with more status conscious neighbors. What we give in money we get back in the experiences that money buys. What the monetarily rich get in money, they provide in experiences to the outside world, directly or indirectly. The more valuably, network-encapsulatingly abstract one's field, the more money society tends to pay them.

If only those of us among the monetarily non-rich could tap into this secret—where sufficient money-capital eludes us, the experiences which that money capital would buy (if we had it) might arrive in piles. But monetary acquisition is an exercise in objective value trading. Not all of us are fundamentally interested or invested enough in the language of abstracted objects to play that game successfully. Fortunately, there are at least three alternatives to money capitalism from which we can build the same wealthy endings. They are

Social capital – where the person wealthy in this way can easily interact with people to trade in experiences most people couldn't otherwise access. He may not have the money to purchase the yacht, but he has friends who will let him sail along with them whenever. Being attractive, working in the service industry, and having some obviously usable talent in others' eyes all contribute to a person's having naturally high social capital. Think about why this might be. And no, having a lot of money *does not* guarantee a lot of social capital. As many among the rich will attest, there's a difference between friends who like being connected to you, and hires who like being paid by you.

Emotional capital – where the person wealthy in this way can easily trade in fulfillment, a sense of empowerment, or any other emotion. He may not have the money to purchase the yacht, but then again he has the inner feeling of sailing free no matter *where* you put him. Artists, musicians, teachers, and people who love doing things for larger society tend to have higher emotional capital. Regardless of what pays better, many of these will have prized their inner expression—projected into a usefulness clearly beyond themselves—much more than those who've felt stakeholder-obligated by the paycheck.

Psychological capital – where the person wealthy in this way can easily trade in behaviors, pulling them out or projecting them onto people and events with free license. He may not have the money to purchase the yacht, but he has a quality which gives him the yacht-sailing role among his peers. Athletes, people with a talent for leading or commanding, and others who have clear knowledge of their own talents tend to have higher psychological capital. Whenever they do what they do, the fact that most others couldn't do it is evident.

Now I can imagine someone facetiously saying, "All that sounds nice, but I'd rather have the money." And maybe that's true. For some of us, money is naturally more favorable than the experiences it buys (emotional), the people we share its purchases with or sources we purchase from (social), or our ability to live in the ways those purchased experiences suggest we that live (psychological). But perhaps you can see how, in some cases, any one of these expressions is no good without the others. You bought the boat with money, but found it a pain to maintain psychologically. You bought the mansion with money, but it's not as fun as the apartment you shared with friends socially. Other forms of capital matter. People who have plenty of money know this. Those of us preoccupied with its attainment tend not to.

The Purpose of This Book

The purpose of this book is to walk you through the development of non-capital wealth. Money is important. We get it. But chances are your life is full of objects which reflect the money you've made over the years—things you wanted and eventually got—but there may still be sides of yourself which you're still seeking to release. We're taught that money will enable such release, but maybe that's an exaggeration of money's power. After all, you finally did get that phone didn't you? Have you released that "whatever-it-is" yet? How about the money you earned last year and the year before that? Are you high on life like the emotionally wealthy person yet? Are you surrounded with people who fill your life with great echoes of the things you love and love to do? Wasn't money said to be a way of getting you there? But we know money doesn't work like that. It's just a unit of account, a store of value, and a medium of exchange. It's just traded effort in publicly recognizable form. If you haven't learned to put the energy you've been given towards uses that fulfill you, tomorrow's money won't fulfill you either. This book aims to help you get past that barrier.

References

keep a ready place   1

Elias, R. Z., & Farag, M. (2010). The relationship between accounting students' love of money and their ethical perception. *Managerial Auditing Journal, 25*, 269–281.

a store of value   2

Krugman, P., Wells, R. & Graddy, K. (2010). *Essentials of economics.* Worth.

can be thought of as the "energy carrier"   3

Ferreira, J. C., & Martins, A. L. (2018). Building a community of users for open market energy. *Energies, 11*(9), 2330.

but the work we'll need to put in   3

Alagidede, P. (2012). Trends and cycles in the net barter terms of trade for Sub-Saharan Africa's primary commodity exporters. *Journal of Developing Areas, 46*(2), 213–229.

...the resources we use are scarce   4

Barnett, H. (1979). Scarcity and growth revisited. *Scarcity and growth Reconsidered,* 163-217.

Meuris, J., & Leana, C. R. (2015). The high cost of low wages: Economic scarcity effects in organizations. *Research in Organizational Behavior, 35*, 143-158.

Bowring, F. (1999). Job scarcity: The perverted form of a potential blessing. *Sociology, 33*(1), 069-084.

Benson, B. L. (1998). Economic freedom and the evolution of law. *CATO Journal, 18*(2), 209.

Wong, M. Y. H. (2017). Helping the rich get richer: A re-assessment of the income distributional trend in Hong Kong. *Asian Studies Review, 41*(2), 191–208.

Vaheesan, S. (2019). Accommodating capital and policing labor: Antitrust in the two gilded ages. *Maryland Law Review, 78*(4), 766–827.

Persky, J. (2018). Say's Law, Marxian crisis theory and the interconnectedness of the capitalist economy. *Review of Political Economy, 30*(3), 269–283.

socially responsible leanings won't reduce   5
Crewe, L. (2000). Progress reports, geographies of retailing and consumption. *Progress in Human Geography, 24*(2), 275–290.

who are monetarily dependent   5
Block, F. (1977). The ruling class does not rule: Notes on the Marxist theory of the state. *Socialist Revolution, 33*(7).

have also made the power structures   5
Matveev, I. (2019). Big business in Putin's Russia: Structural and instrumental power. *Demokratizatsiya, 27*(4), 401–422.

become poorer in political mobility   6
Ruggera, L., & Barone, C. (2017). Social closure, micro-class immobility and the intergenerational reproduction of the upper class: a comparative study. *British Journal of Sociology, 68*(2), 194–214.

a conjecture on...a widening wealth gap   6
Alfani, G. (2010). Wealth inequalities and population dynamics in early modern Northern Italy. *Journal of Interdisciplinary History, 40*(4), 513–549.

it must adopt a...subscription path   6
Applequist, J., & Ball, J. G. (2018). An updated analysis of direct-to-consumer television advertisements for prescription drugs. *Annals of Family Medicine, 16*(3), 211–216.

Karl Marx would have said   6
Sperber, J. (2013). Karl Marx the German. *German History, 31*(3), 383–402.

WITHOUT the aid of the rest   7
Levi, P. (2009). Our path: Against Putschism. *Historical Materialism, 17*(3), 111–145.

A slave with the freedom   7
Kucukaydin, I. (2010). Counter-learning under oppression. *Adult Education Quarterly, 60*(3), 215–232.

Uber vs—   8
Griffith, K. (2019). The Uber loophole that protects surge pricing. *Virginia Journal of Social Policy & the Law, 26*(1), 35–64.

the consumer's need for a choice between   8
Mick, D. G., & Fournier, S. (1998). Paradoxes of technology: Consumer cognizance, emotions, and coping strategies. *Journal of Consumer Research, 25*(2), 123–143.

maybe because it looked the part   9

Genschow, O., Demanet, J., Hersche, L., & Brass, M. (2017). An empirical comparison of different implicit measures to predict consumer choice. *PLoS ONE, 12*(8), 1–13.

Social capital   10

Adler, S. P.; Kwon, S. K. (2002). Social capital: Prospects for a new concept. *Academy of Management Review, 27*, 17–40.

Emotional capital   11

Thagard, P. (2015). Emotional capital. *Psychology Today*. Retrieved January 6, 2020 from https://www.psychologytoday.com/us/blog/hot-thought/201509/emotional-capital

Psychological capital   11

Luthans, F., Youssef-Morgan, C. M., & Avolio, B. (2007). *Psychological capital: Developing the human competitive edge*. Oxford University Press.

Chapter 2: The Four Forms of Capital

It's about now that I'd like to undo what I've been referring to as "rich" versus "non-rich." I've been framing these in the monetary sense with the according connotations, but on the most basic level we know that riches are relative. A couple that has saved up $750,000 might seem super rich to a person who only has $57 in his bank account. But if that couple still owes $490,000 on their house and $190,000 in other ongoing debts, a debt free person who has saved up $90,000 might actually seem better off. This can hold true even if the actual numbers don't add up. Surely we all know this. And then there are people who are worth millions or even billions, who simply aren't satisfied. They might have high monetary capital with comparatively lower psychological capital than their lower-middle class peers. All of this prompts us to reconsider what it means to think of someone as being "rich."

For the purposes of developing the non-capital sides of wealth, we'll need a usable definition of riches. But before we settle on such a definition, we'll need a much better sense of what constitutes capital.

It's unfortunate that monetary wealth has such an easy reference object for insinuating itself into our thoughts: money. That is, it's easy to think of wealth in the monetary sense because it's easy to think of monetary and capital currency: The vehicle for monetary wealth is money[1]—something we can easily picture, count, and reference. But if money is the currency of monetary capital, what are the currencies of social, psychological, and emotional capital? We want to define riches, but we need to know what it means to be rich in these areas beyond the capital. If you're rich in social capital for example, what is it that you have a lot of?

Capital Wealth

Let's define monetary riches as having a lot of money. That's a start. Now we just need to know what "having," "a lot," and "money" each mean. We'll see shortly why it's useful to break up our definition like this. Assume the following:

---

[1] Money is considered the main engine of monetary capital, though its more abstract forms like credit, stock, holdings, commodified currency, and the right to convey (options) are also related forms of money.

- **having** means (physically, psychologically, socially, or emotionally) possessing access to the immediate experience of a thing *in the way you want to experience it*. Being able to look at it under glass isn't the same as having it. You need access in the way *you want* to access it.

- **a lot** means (psychologically, socially, or emotionally) considering that there is much more of something than is needed for the purpose at hand.

- **money** as we defined earlier consisted of a store of value, a unit of account, and a medium of exchange. We'll broadly summarize this as the abstractified (publicly-recognized) value used for trading in objects. "Abstractified value" for short.

  o Here, an object could be a thing, service, or any other fixed construct whose "thingness" the trading parties can agree on. That part is important, because when the parties can't agree on what's being traded or can't agree on the value that the traded thing represents, money will ultimately fall in usefulness.

We also note that money is the <u>unit</u> of monetary riches. When a person has monetary riches PLUS access to the kind of lifestyle those riches are expected to buy, that person has monetary **wealth**. That is,

- Riches means having a lot of a thing

- Wealth means having a lot of a thing along with access to the situations that thing can be used to acquire. Said differently, wealth is the same as "tier-usuable riches;" where the riches you have can be used to buy things that come with the public expectations of the value tier you're on.

  A person with ten million dollars who's only ever in a position to buy bread and water would be considered rich but not wealthy in terms of what the rest of us expect ten million dollars to buy.

When we add in things like people (as **bodies**, not relationships), **land**, **holdings**, **labor**, and **credit**—allowing these to be traded interchangeably for money—the collection of all these money-tradable classes is called **(monetary) capital**. From here on we can no longer simply talk about monetary value, but now have to talk about broader capital value. If monetary riches means having a lot of money, capital riches means having a lot of capital. **Capital wealth** means having a lot of access to the kinds of situations that capital riches can buy.

Before we move on let's note a couple of things about money—especially for those of us who haven't had the best relationship with it.

Money is the currency for trading objects or opportunities whose forms we can agree on. It is the quickest, broadest, most useful means of translating one person's value for an object into another's value for that same object. Some people think you need money to live, but most children don't have very much money and they still live. Certain homeless, very low-income social tiers, maintained spouses and relatives on every economic level, and societies under distress can *and do* make it without meaningful money of their own. The more you are provided for by sources who will give you the agreed upon objects, the lower your need for money. So you don't actually *need* money to live. You *strongly prefer* to have money to live *as you wish* and trade the objects *of your choosing*. That's different. The more you exaggerate the importance of money next to things like breathing air and keeping healthy relationships along with the money you have, the harder it will be for you to enjoy the other three kinds of wealth.

Money is not the root of all evil. Again, you probably know this. But if that statement forms a real fixture in your outlook towards money, then it will be harder for you to address the actual psychological and relational areas of your life where things that truly are "evil" to you really do arise. We will be developing our skills in non-capital wealth, but in order to do so we'll really need to keep money in its proper place. Even if we only say it jokingly, claiming that money is the root of all evil is more of a reflection of our unwillingness to dig any further than fixed objects for the cause of our problems dynamically relating to what we want. Psychological and social capital in particular will be that much harder to build up to wealthy levels.

As I mentioned earlier, part of the reason we are able to inflate the importance of monetary measure above and beyond psychological, emotional, and social health is because—unlike these other three—monetary measure has an easily recognizable currency in the form of money. In order to give these other areas the weight they deserve, it would be helpful for us to recognize the currency specific to each as well as the reasons why money would be no substitute for these other currencies. Let's get started.

A Definition of Capital

In the same way that a state capital administers the business of an entire state, general capital can be thought of in terms of the "states" its prime currency trades in. Our regular notion of (monetary) capital translates fixed(ish)-agreed public objects into various states of money—including land and labor. In this way, capital can be thought of as "the collection of things that can be practically converted into the same specific currency." (Monetary) capital is the collection of things that can be practically converted into money. Given this, we can ask what constitutes the other three forms of capital. That is, these are collections of things that can be practically converted into *what*?

Psychological Capital

If **money** trades in [**public** ✓**value-agreeable**], [**public** ✓**form-agreeable**] objects, what happens when we *can't* agree on the ✗value but *can* agree on the ✓form? For example, what if we know what a skilled leader looks like, but have no reasonable way of agreeing on what the worth of that leader might be? My definition of a leader might be my late dad. Your definition might be Genghis Khan. If I need you to be a leader in the truly non-commodifiable, invaluable sense, how can I ever pay you commensurate with your ability to motivate people from within? Typically I can't. The best I can do is hire a manager and put "Dad- or Genghis Khan-like" in the job description, and assign a worth relative to the rest of my company. But perhaps you can see how this might be a pitiful failure on my part to bring a real leader to my company. Especially if the hired person's inspirational motivation is contingent on the money I pay him. Where forcing value onto an invaluable role only serves to limit that role, we can only expect so much from money. We'll need to trade in psychologies. We might have an easier time finding a leader in exchange for a "bold opportunity" or a tractable "system of followers" than we would with money. Enter the realm of psychological capital.

If people rich in money have a lot of access to the units of trading objects, people rich in psychology have a lot of access to the units of role performance. Rather than drawing upon the tools for buying porsches and yachts, they can draw upon the tools for affecting situations as teachers, leaders, servants, or superstars. Whatever role you put them in, they can easily figure out how to live it. In this way, the psychologically rich person is broadly effective. Thus, the currency of psychological capital is role efficacy[2] (or efficacy for short). The psychologically wealthy feel they can accomplish any task set before them, put on any mask, and create meaningful experiences wherever you put them.

In my younger years I often asked why so many celebrities seemed to be dissatisfied with their lives even amidst their stardom. I later realized that celebs aren't gods. They're just humans like the rest of us. Possible monetary riches aside, there are industry mechanics, privacy threats, performance restrictions, and even indenture-type agreements which can rob a money rich person of their ability to control the circumstances which provide that money, up to and including their basic individual behaviors. The monetarily non-rich and general public may be shocked to learn that money did not equal complete happiness for

---

[2] The more generally accepted definition of psychological capital also includes facets such as hope, optimism, resiliency, and various other forms of satisfaction. Because we'll be framing this in terms of tradeable economics however, I'm grouping these under various forms of past, present, future-expectant, and situational-sustaining "efficacy."

the former, but as I mentioned earlier, the higher you rise, the more fixed expectations for what got you there. Money can buy the tangibles, but once you've bought all of the tangibles that really interest you, then what? If only we could use money to buy money-resistant role expression, maybe much of this would cease to be a problem. But money isn't that useful for measuring things resistant to measurement.

Efficacy is the currency of psychological capital. Anything performance-, individual motivation-, and unique personality-related will tend to require psychological capital for trading. Just as monetary capital includes money, land, and labor for example, psychological capital also comes in multiple forms

- General efficacy – skill in any situation. This is the main currency of psychological capital.

- Specific efficacy – skill in a particular niche or arena of talent. Championship teams assemble specific members towards the building of a generally winning group.

- Tractability – the ability to receive an effective person's skills. Where our company is looking for a leader, we promise you a staff who will carry out your vision to its utmost.

• Expertise – the situational *foundations* for being effective in a particular place. In exchange for your artistic talents, we'll give you access to all the software and imaging gadgets you could ever want.

Perhaps you can see how monetary capital might actually be more expensive, less long-term motivating, and less short-term efficient than psychological capital in compensating a person for the invaluable role you wish them to perform.   More than just being true for companies, this is especially true for our peers on a project and things we do with others to express ourselves for fun. Personality-rich people need circumstances which enable them. No amount of money can secure their loyalty to the cause, even if it can secure their continued employment.

Social Capital

Most of us are familiar with the phrase, "It's who you know." Realistically it's more like "who you know and who likes you (or your skills)." When we can agree on the ✓value, but can't agree on the ✗form, we set up a trade in a series of objects which are never the same. These aren't actually objects though. They're more like relationships. Relationships are the currency of social capital, and constitute the #1 determinant of wishes granted to you by other parties in places where even money (believe it or not) becomes too inconvenient.

The problem with a lot of our relationships is that we attempt to commodify them. What *could be* an ongoing exchange of interests and talents becomes a boxed event with some kind of price tag on it. So I'll take you places if you give me gas money every time. No gas money, no transportation. Now, arrangements like this may or may not be appropriate in certain cases for you as a reader, and a lot of that depends on the level of trust (or utility) between you and the other parties. In general though, the difference between [having a relationship with] and [being a frequent customer of] someone is that, in the former case the price is continued access to another party's world; in the latter case the price is paid one stoppable event at a time, with less of that access guaranteed by either party (lest it become exploitative).

But where we *trade in monetary capital despite social capital being more appropriate*, we end up with two side effects:

Trust between parties tends to be lower in the monetary case, and will often need to be further secured through various third-party mediated contracts (ironically social in connection, as in the messaged promise everyone knows you made).

Above-and-beyond behavior is far less likely by the party receiving the fee, and additional exchange-building behavior is less likely by the party paying the fee, as both of these cases often change the rate automatically. Where we expect (or even require) the cooperation of another beyond the contractual letter—where we expect them to still be okay with us were the situation to change even a little, social capital forms a vitally important companion to monetary capital. Indeed, one of the whole aims of branding something is to attach socialized differentiation to an otherwise generic commodity.

The overall rule for social capital is as follows:

If you expect or want the exchange to be ongoing,

if you'd rather trade up front for access to something that will probably be different every time,

if you want to build trust with the other party—where each can assume the other won't vacate once payment stops,

if you yourself would rather "pay" in forms that change—sometimes in gas money, sometimes in companionship, then

social capital is likely a better unit of exchange than monetary capital.

Money is better for quick, convenient, utilitarian excursions to some kind of "store," where there is low uncertainty in what's being traded or for how long. We have many transactions that work this way, but our most important transactions go far beyond this— necessitating a more appropriate value carrier.

Social capital's multiple forms have been formally described as bonding, bridging and linking. But because these do not take nearly as much account of the more neutral to negative-seeming relationships which are nevertheless essential to our definition as capital actors, we'll need to reframe these to fit a more you-centered perspective and then add a fourth (clarifying relationships) as a way of explaining those associations we have whose value isn't comfortably felt unless we frame our worlds *against* them.

- Beneficial relationships – patterns of exchange which help us access what we want to access; these are aimed at the positive present and future

- Defensive relationships – patterns of exchanges which protect us from things we *don't want* accessing us; these are typically aimed at the non-negative present and future

- Clarifying relationships – patterns of exchange which help us know or find what we want, even if they don't help us access those things. These are often the best final form of our relationships with enemies, and are often aimed at transitioning or assessing the present, or solidifying the results of past decisions.

- Familiar relationships – patterns of exchange which remind us of what we can currently access even if our experiences have helped convince us otherwise; these are aimed at recovering the past through the present, building on the life histories and psychologies available to us.

Notice that social capital isn't just about who can hook you up with the sweet life. It's also about who can hook you up with a life which is more "you" than the more generic world has been able to teach. It is especially important to notice that not all of your social assets will be friends. Sports teams need opponents. Liberators need oppressors. Kings need citizens. You're probably socially richer than you know, if only you knew what your ideal social role actually was.

Emotional Capital

To the extent that most of us know a great deal about what we like emotionally, most of us already have plenty of emotional capital. Its currency is called fulfillment. Fulfillment of our wants. Since almost any action we take can present us with some form of fulfillment somewhere, we can be thought of as having an endless store of emotional capital right up until the day we die. Among all the forms of capital, the emotional kind is the only one which is NEVER EVER SCARCE—even if your form of fulfillment is to remain familiarly depressed.[3] And that fact will be instrumental

---

[3] Psychological capital is also highly resistant to scarcity.

in our framing of non-capital alternatives to exchange later on. For now though, we'll consider this last source of capital to be rooted in the feeling that one's aims have been met. A person rich in emotional capital has the capacity to feel fulfilled beyond necessity (for continuing the event) in a lot of situations, and is able to draw on this in his various doings. In other scholarly settings we might say the amount of "emotional labor" he requires to manage his feelings to his liking is reasonably light.

Now there's good news and bad news regarding emotional capital. Since we all have it, it's not really a matter of getting more. It's more a matter being in the right situation to acknowledge such fulfillment in the right kinds of ways. That's the good news. But if money trades in public value-agreeable, public form-agreeable objects, what happens when we can agree on the desirability of fulfillment but not on the form that fulfillment takes in each personality? What if we also can't agree on how much fulfillment is enough for the parties involved?

When we can *neither agree on the ×form nor the ×value* of what we intend to trade, all we have are intentions (motives). Trading in motives means that we'll definitely need to adopt trading partners or situations who adopt the language of our likes. In this way, most of us are by default at the mercy of what we've been *taught to like*—dedicating our emotional capital to the not-necessarily optimal *familiar* things, chief among which is the striving for more monetary and psychological capital as advertised by the world around us. Rich in dormant emotional capital, most of us don't know what to do with the patterns of fulfillment we carry. We have the capital, but don't know how to trade it or who to trade it with. That's the bad news. If you think about it, you could be a billionaire who doesn't recognize his or her ongoing, money-independent access to the experiences that fulfill you, where much of the money is just extra.

We're taught that the next purchase will make us feel better and more secure, and each time we believe that message to be the case, the money we would spend on that purchase goes out the window. Does that make sense? Maybe this is easier to see in hindsight. Imagine someone told you that the latest smart watch would really fulfill you. You eventually got the watch, but now months later the thrill has worn off. Your $800 is gone, your fulfillment has subsided, and your $800 is still gone. The money had been a portion of the kind of riches that were supposed to bring some far off happiness to the past version of yourself, but now you've replaced that happily "watched" person with someone who's still looking for more cash. Can you see how money without the ability to be emotionally fulfilled may, in many cases, be the same as no money at all? Especially after that watch ends up in a box in the closet two years later. You asked for it, you got it, and now the whole thing has lost its importance.

The point is not to preach to you. It's only to say that emotional capital is something we take for granted. Unable to make use of it, all the other forms of capital assume a level of importance that may not actually be necessary for our psychologically wealthy lives. More money so we can buy more experiences with which we could have more emotionally fulfilling times among more emotionally fulfilling friends and environments. But people who are emotionally wealthy can access—for virtually free—the things that some people will never find even with billions of dollars at their disposal. If money determines which extra objects we can buy, fulfillment determines our desire to buy them in the first place.

Emotional capital comes in a couple of forms:

- *Fulfillment* – seeing what one has as being plenty; related to a reference situation

- *Satisfaction* – not needing more; related to oneself *despite* a reference situation

So when do we actually trade in emotional capital? Mainly when we've settled on something for the long term.

When either you or your trading partner stops caring about the details of your exchange,

when you stop counting or keeping score,

when, no matter what the form, you simply won't tolerate a certain thing anymore,

when you've decided that a certain area of uncertainty should actually fit you over the long term,

you might be better served to trade in emotional capital.

True friends, things you're a fan of, lifestyle habits like collections and travel preferences, your life ambitions, or general identity constructs are all better served by emotional trading because of their ongoing reflections of who you are over entire changeable domains of action. <u>Putting yourself in situations that match you</u> is the name of the game, and from there your trading partners become the givers or receivers of your continued fulfillment.

The Difference between Social and Emotional Capital

In the case of friends, social capital and emotional capital can be easily confused, but aren't the same. We have high social capital when we have lots of beneficial relationships, but if those relationships aren't fulfilling— maybe they continually convince us to chase more than is there—then they don't represent emotional capital. On the other hand, many people have low social capital—not a lot of beneficial relationships, but are instead dependent on one or two people to provide for them; if these beneficiaries don't want for anything more than this, being largely fulfilled in this arrangement, then they will still have high emotional capital for drawing on their fulfillment needs.

Summary

In this chapter we've outlined four forms of capital and why money is an inefficient substitute for the other three when we're dealing with immeasurable amounts or changeable forms in the objects of trade. Try as we may to attach dollars to phenomena like fulfillment, relationships, and role efficacy, we're never really very good at it. Using money to exchange these things almost always brings us face to face with the limits on what we actually want.

Now that we've seen the different kinds of capital, we'll move on to discuss the idea of transactions and why it actually takes two forms of capital for us to get any good trading done. Stay tuned.

References

When we add in things like people   22
Krugman, P., Wells, R. & Graddy, K. (2010). *Essentials of economics*. Worth.

when we can't agree on the value but   25
Grant, J. (2014). *Seeking talent for creative cities*. University of Toronto Press.

an easier time finding a leader   26

Wang, L., & Long, L. (2018). Idiosyncratic deals and taking charge: The roles of psychological empowerment and organizational tenure. *Social Behavior & Personality: An International Journal, 46*(9), 1437–1448.

the currency of psychological capital   27

Ohlin, B. (2019). Psycap 101: Your guide to increasing psychological capital. Retrieved January 6, 2020 from https://positivepsychology.com/psychological-capital-psycap/

Relationships are the currency   30

Claride, T. (2013). Explanation of types of social capital. *Social Capital Research & Training.* Retrieved January 6, 2020 from https://www.socialcapitalresearch.com/explanation-types-social-capital/

two side effects   30
bonding, bridging and linking   32

OECD n.d. What is social capital? Retrieved January 6, 2020 from https://www.oecd.org

(or even require) the cooperation of another   31

Hamilton, K., Helliwell, J. F., and Woolcock, M. (2016). Social capital, trust and well-being in the evaluation of wealth. *NBER Working Paper Series, 22556.*

the amount of "emotional labor" he requires   35
Hochschild, A. R. (1983). *The managed heart: Commercialization of human feeling.* Berkeley. University of California Press.

to acknowledge such fulfillment   35
Mastracci, S., & Adams, I. (2018). "That's what the money's for": Alienation and emotional labor in public service. *Administrative Theory & Praxis, 40*(4), 304–319.

can be easily confused   39
Hayat, N. (2010). Evaluation of human capital. *SSRN.* Retrieved January 6, 2020 from https://ssrn.com/abstract=1667294

Chapter 3: Trading in Twos

There is a well-known model in economics called the circular flow model which describes the path of goods, services, and capital in an economic system. Briefly summarized, the model maintains that households, businesses, product markets, resource markets, and governments all participate in a chain of transactions which keep (mainly monetary) capital flowing in exchange for the various demands of each system. We won't go into the details of this, but the model is summarized in Figure 3.1 below.

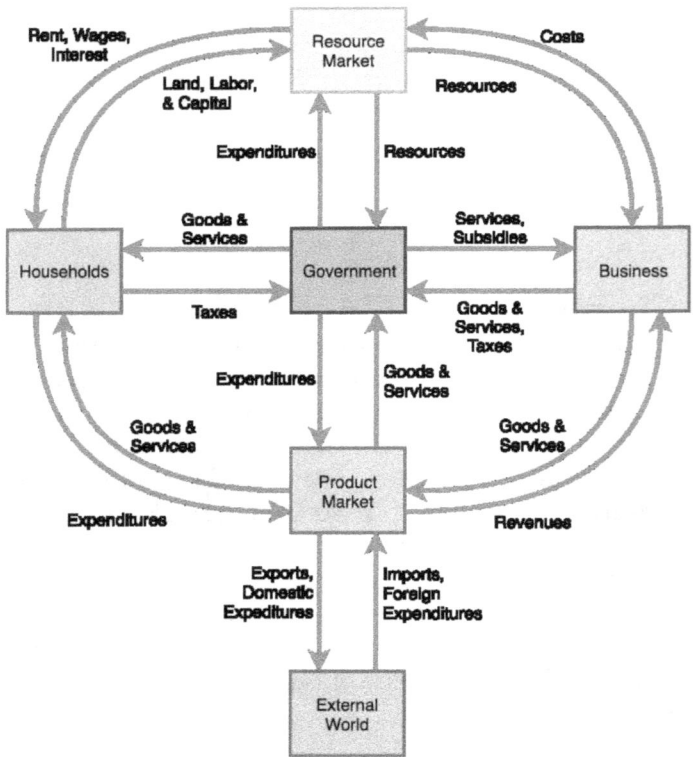

Figure 3.1. The circular flow model
for an economic system

For our purposes, the picture may be more
useful than the economics itself, mainly
because the picture provides us with a
valuable tool for considering where the other

three forms of capital fit into the rest of the economic scene.

While the circular flow model surely provides a valuable tool for tracking money through a system, perhaps you can see how it omits most of the details regarding what actually goes on in a person's house. With all of our talk about jobs, for example, you would think that this kind of model would address the availability of employment in the resource market, the role of payable skills in various areas, the different levels of government for those who pay into the Kingdom Homeowners association and those who don't. But then again that's probably asking too much from something that was really meant to provide just an overview.

Still, when we introduce jobs, skills, and standards of living into this well-known economic model, we start to see the holes in its ability to describe our everyday lives. The circular flow model of economics treats wages and labor as if they are equally translatable into capital, for example. Translatable they may be, but not equally so. For it is in the changing nature of labor previously nonexistent in a system that entire fields of expertise such as data science and biotech may emerge from "nowhere" in the economic map. In times of financial panic, more of the capital may flow into mattress savings, but there is no indication in the model for the well-studied role of public emotions in a state's economic stability. What I want to convince you of is that our normal models of economics have always had social, psychological, and emotional factors built into them, though these are traditionally framed in terms of capital and (perhaps unfortunately) are not given names in classical models like these. And although it probably isn't practical to alter the circular flow model to account for non-capital processes, it is worth observing that those processes are there, they directly affect you, and (if you can develop your talent for using them) those processes can be used to build up your wealth in several areas, not just monetarily.

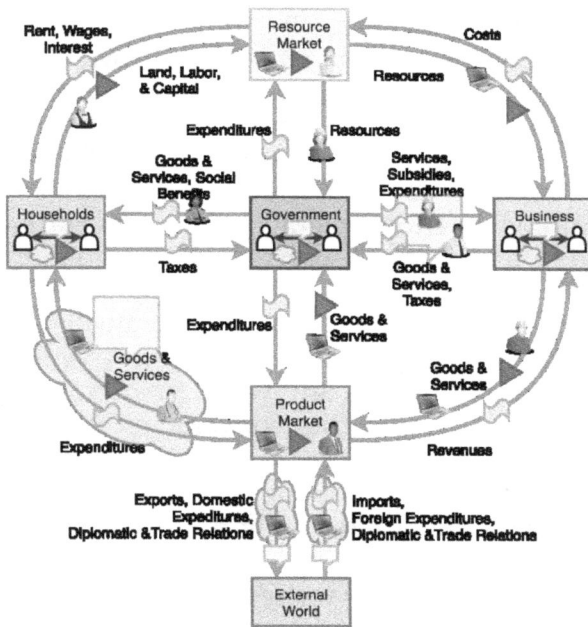

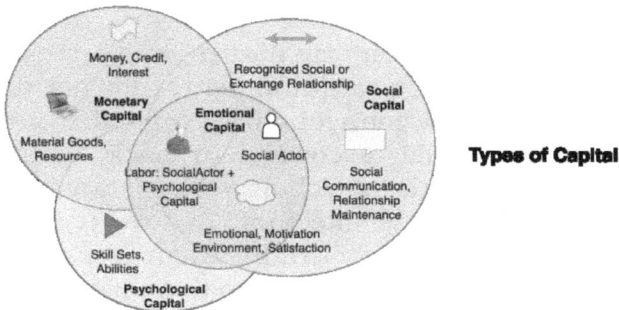

Figure 3.2. A circular flow model with non-monetary elements added.

Barring interest, the financial, and the currency markets, it should be obvious that we don't typically trade money for money. Usually we trade money for goods and services. Businesses trade money for skills and labor. Citizens of a state trade money for a kind of civic fulfillment (police powers, paved roads, and other services that satisfy our needs for a certain tolerable lifestyle). For every transaction we enter, we typically trade something we're willing to part with for something different we wish to obtain. And although it might be convenient for us to think of the objects we buy as being equivalent to the monetary-capital we pay for them, we individuals rarely buy them for their capital value (unless we're investing). Instead, the things we purchase like food, clothes, and internet service are typically bought for the experiences they enable—necessity or not. Food is not monetary by nature, but serves as a source of biological fulfillment. Internet is a means to social connection. Beyond the basic collection needed to cover your back, clothes can be identity-psychological, statement-social, or anything like that, but we typically don't buy them to trade them for other objects. That is, they aren't monetary by nature. What does all of this mean? It means you've probably been using your monetary capital to buy non-monetary experiences all along. To the extent that much of the money wealth you've already earned in the past has been converted to experiences sponsored by the things bought, much of your economic life has likely been spent trading capital wealth for non-capital wealth in the form of fulfilled health, effective action histories, and social memories.

Money is important as abstractified currency, but much of the purpose in our making it is for us to trade it for non-monetary things and events. Our aim for the rest of this book will be learning how to build those non-monetary experiences in ways that can supplement or even replace an explicitly money-capital transaction.

References

circular flow model   43

Cohen, J. (1963). Circular flow models in the flow of funds. *International Economic Review, 4*(2), 153-170.

Krugman, P., Wells, R. & Graddy, K. (2010). *Essentials of economics*. Worth.

may emerge from "nowhere"   45

Song, D., Liu, S., & Shi, H. (2015). Formation mechanism and evolutionary path of emerging industries. *Journal of Grey System, 27*(3), 203–212.

may flow into mattress savings   46

Ramírez, C. D. (2009). Bank fragility, "money under the mattress", and long-run growth: US evidence from the "perfect" Panic of 1893. *Journal of Banking & Finance, 33*(12), 2185–2198.

we don't typically trade money for money   48

O'Shaughnessy, J. (1992). *Explaining buyer behavior*. Oxford University Press.

Chapter 4: Monetary Capital

Despite the stories we tell ourselves about the kinds of rich lives we would live if we had the money, the reality is that most us would likely only live shinier versions of the lives we currently live. Among the non-rich, there is a tendency to say things like, "One day I'll buy that big house"—the assumption being that such a moment in time (the moment of purchase) would bring us fulfillment for the future thereafter. Yet our lives prove otherwise time and again:

1. Today I don't have what I want.

2. Tomorrow I'll get it, then I'll be happy. (Supposedly every day after that?)

3. Some time passes. I get what I wanted.

4. I'm happy for that day.

1. More time passes. Today I don't have what I want.

And what do we learn from all this? We learn that the things we want may not be as significant as the *ways* in which we want them, and how we spend our time in light of doing so. During the wanting period, our psychologies engage in a pattern of seeking and desiring, interfacing with various others in order to bring about not only the thing we want, but many other things in between. Very rarely does that dream purchase, dream gift, or dream toy deliver on its promise over the time following its occurrence. The exception to this tends to be events or trips which are truly one of a kind. The difference between the object-like moments we seek to buy and the efficacy-like events we wish to extend is that the former require our psychologies to extract their use while the latter, by their nature, steer our psychologies to fit a scenario. That is,

> Future purchases will grant different levels of satisfaction depending on how active we are in engaging them.

> Future purchases will grant different time spans of satisfaction depending on how reflective they are of our long term patterns of "fulfillment behavior."

If it has always been your dream to collect 1000 purple Hot Wheels cars, purchasing them may actually fulfill you over the long term. But if it's only your current dream to buy a newer bigger house, purchasing that house will only fulfill you until you want a bigger, newer house again or decide to downsize. When we talk about the kinds of things we would do if we had more money, we often assume that anything we'd buy would bring some kind of fulfillment over the *long-ish term* thereafter. We conveniently forget that the same pattern of complaints, dissatisfaction, strained relationships, and inconsistent preferences we have now will also follow us into that future. If you've complained about things breaking down in the last two houses you've had, what makes you think you won't complain when they break down in your mansion? If you're annoyed at the inconvenience of going through the airport now, what makes you think you won't be annoyed on that trip to Fiji later?

The point is not to burst your bubble. In this chapter we'll actually work on clarifying how you would *really* spend your capital wealth if you had all the money capital you ever needed. But we need to start by dispelling the myth that objects we want today won't become the same objects we're tired of tomorrow. It's not the tradable objects we're interested in. It's the experiences those objects bring. Once we've identified the experiences, we'll ask whether they are psychological, social, or emotional in nature. From there we'll look at where those experiences are mirrored in the lives we currently lead, in order to simulate the kind of capital prosperity we want. Lastly, we'll take a look at how our psychologies change as this simulated monetary capital arrives, noting the things we do differently which go hand in hand with our more monetarily prosperous selves.

Tracing the Psychology behind Your Capital Wealth

Keeping in mind what we talked about at the beginning of this chapter, answer the following question: What would you do if you had all the money you ever needed to do anything you ever wanted? (Be warned, this question has consequences. So be realistic!)

Try to list at least four or five dream goals if you can think of them.

And now for an important follow up item: For every item you put in the box above, why would you do it? That is, what experience would you be going for?

Next, an even more important follow up question: **For every item you put in the first box how will you deal with the** people **affected by your decision?** If you said you would buy an island for example, how would you handle the people already on that island? If the island were deserted, how would you locate it to begin with? Who would you charter with to travel out there and build on it? Who would build on it? If you said you would throw grand parties on the island every day, who would you invite? Would you invite people who wouldn't give you the time of day if you *didn't* own the island? Strange people who owned the islands nearby? Do you do that kind of thing with neighbors or co-workers now? Again, the point isn't to burst your bubble. It's to get you thinking about how your real and current psychology would play out if you actually got your wish in real life. You do want it in real life, don't you?

Last question. **Given what you'd do, why, and with whom, what would you find the most fulfilling about each thing you listed?** This is critically important for the rest of the exercise. If you said you'd buy a Maserati, is it because you'd be fulfilled by the status of owning a brand named, expensive sports car? Would you be fulfilled by the feeling of being different and uninhibited compared to everyone else?

Whatever you put in the box above tells you more about what your subconscious actually wants from the objects of boundless trade. Consider whether these things are social, emotional, or psychological in nature.

If you had the money, you would trade it for...

We've now asked what we would do if money were no object. But we didn't stop at dreams. We brought those dreams down to practical reality by looking at how our actual personalities would work with the details of those dreams. We asked what the point of each dream was in the first place. We asked how those dreams fulfilled us. Was that car the completion of a childhood fantasy, or was it status-based ego fulfillment? Let's take the answers from that last question and translate them into more long-term processes. You'll see where we're going with this shortly.

Given your answers to the last question in the previous section, turn your answers into generic "I like" statements (if you dare). When I did this exercise, for example, one of my dreams was to build an educational theme park. I'd ask my friends to help me find the people to build it. That's because I love the human dynamic. And the most fulfilling part would be the ability to share, in a wondrous way, the subjects I'm so passionate about. My "I like" statement would thus be, "I love sharing, in a wondrous way, the subjects I'm so passionate about." If your "I like" statement doesn't really suit you, you don't have to put it down. You might take a second look at your dream goals, though.

So now you have not only a list of psychological favorites, but likely a list of emotional favorites as well. If you were clear enough in your goals, you should have produced at least a couple of experiences which are long-term appealing for you as an economic actor. If there were a store you could visit in order to buy your "I likes," you might camp out there. Next we'll ask a context question.

For each of your "I likes," where in your daily life do you get the opportunity to do it easily and regularly? If you can't do it presently, where have you best been able to do it in the past?

Among what kinds of people or personalities?

What kind of role have you traditionally held when doing these things?

**For each of your "I like" roles, in what
ways does the situation you've described
differ from the opportunities available to
you now?**

And there you have it. The actual super
money-rich lifestyle cast in terms of the
psychology you'd use those riches to reinforce.
Of course there are many other things you
might do if you won the Powerball, but what
you've listed above stands to be more
consistent in you no matter how much money
you have. These also tend to constitute the set
of events that WON'T come to you just
because you suddenly have the money.

Take a look at the above experiences you've
listed. Not what you expected of capital wealth
were they? That's because money capital
trades in objects. A long-term rich lifestyle
trades in a pattern of events. Even if buying
new objects is a large part of the fun in money
wealth, a string of such purchases invariably

stops looking like individual shopping events and starts looking more like a pattern of *wants* on your behalf (that is, a lifestyle). In order to more realistically know what kind of ongoing life the acquisition of capital wealth would bring us, we've put in some work to identify what our ongoing emotional and psychological priorities were.

On a Collection You Didn't Know You Had

One last picture of monetary capital is a bit unusual. It concerns the arrival of value to you, how you respond to it, and why it takes that form. The idea is, if money trades in objects and certain objects seem to fly at you of their own free will, then even if you're not money-rich, you'll still have a knack for attracting a certain kind of object without trying very hard. Similar to the exercises of the previous section, it is possible for you to repeat the same line of questioning not for what you *would* buy if you were rich, but for what objects actually come to you easily right now. For example,

I have an easy time collecting **clothes** and **video games** from my brothers, **books** and **data** from everyone else. Books in particular have a way of tracking me down and sitting on my shelf; meaningful data patterns have a way of organizing themselves onto my drives. I interact with people who have knowledge that they'd like to give away to anyone who wants it. Let's call these easy collections "uniquely presented perspectives." Because apparently I attract uniquely presented perspectives, the most fulfilling part is adding those quality perspectives to my world view. I love adding quality, humanistic or philosophical perspectives to my worldview, and tend to be a quiet explorer while acquiring these. Psychologically, this suggests that money riches (as **holdings**) may "seek me out" to the extent that I engage in work that gathers "meaningful perspectives" from others.

I could frustrate myself trying to acquire cash, but for me, acquiring cash-tradable data and cash tradable perspective-representation will be (and has been) a lot easier. The result has been a lot of writing about those perspectives and a lot of analysis of those perspectives in a short amount of time, regardless of whether or not the results are ever seen.

What kinds of tradable objects fly at you automatically? They may not be Rolexes, but have you ever wondered what would happen if you actually decided to collect those flying, tradable objects? Doing so engages something that I'll call the **"psychology of easy material acquisition."** Take some time to repeat the exercises in this chapter for the objects that fly in your direction. Note how you behave amidst your own psychology of easy acquisition.

Recap

In this chapter we followed a process for understanding our own approach to money-capital by looking past the purchase, towards the pattern of fulfillment evident in a string of purchases. Some people might be disappointed that we didn't talk about how to become money rich. But the idea here was that money riches by themselves constitute only one half of our limit-defying economic transactions, and that it was more important to work out the fulfillment we intended to gain in spending that money than it was to understand the buildup of money for its own sake. For those interested in the latter, things like status and ego really are legitimate aims, but you can get this without money. Furthermore, I've argued that no matter how much money you have, if you're continually buying things that wear off due to your own habituation to them, you may be throwing your money into a vortex powered by incomplete social, emotional, and psychological aims (unless the thrill is in the shiny newness itself). Is it better to make enough money to buy a new phone, get tired of it, buy a new car, get tired of it, buy another new phone and get tired of it... or is it better to know that keeping up emotionally with the Joneses is priority for you? That depends. In

many cases, though, cutting off the endless
need for more money for more purchases may
easily be a cheaper route if nothing else. It
may be cheaper on you in the long run just to
acknowledge the Joneses and get on with it. In
the meantime, one can get a good sense of
what it's all for with a little bit of
introspection, making it easier for him to see
where that giant house might not be worth it
after all.

I've begun with the psychology of capital
acquisition because I know that many of us
will have difficulty appreciating the non-
capital forms if we don't get this one out of the
way first. Money is important in a world full of
purchasable things, but those purchases—
even when legally required like car
insurance—serve purposes that are not
themselves monetary. They are security- and
socially-, psychology- and compliance-related,
so that we've done some preparatory work in
appreciating the other forms of capital for
which our money will ultimately be traded.

I know a couple of people whose lives are
overwhelmingly dominated by the concern for
money, such that you can never convince
them that there are other vital forms of capital
for which money must be traded. They live in
an eternally unfulfilled, deleterious cycle of

hoped materialism imposed on themselves and others such that you know: no lottery or rich relative will ever buy them out of themselves. It's okay to want money, but not helpful to deny the true value in the things it ultimately trades for. In the next chapter we'll begin exploring those valuable things with a look at the most ubiquitous form of capital of them all: the emotional kind.

References

different levels of satisfaction depending   52
Tan, H. H., Foo, M. D., & Kwek, M. H. (2004). The effects of customer personality traits on the display of positive emotions. *Academy of Management Journal, 47*(2), 287–296.

depending on how reflective they are   52
LaBarbera, P. A., & Mazursky, D. (1983). A longitudinal assessment of consumer satisfaction/dissatisfaction: The dynamic aspect of the cognitive process. *Journal of Marketing Research, 20*(4), 393–404.

the same objects we're tired of tomorrow   53
Wathieu, L. (2004). Consumer habituation. *Management Science, 50*(5), 587–596.

purposes that are not themselves monetary   64

Zymovets, V. V., & Shelud, N. M. (2018). Decapitalization of financial sector: Consequences for the economy of Ukraine. *Economy of Industry, 83*(3), 21–42.

Chapter 5: Emotional Capital

Before we talk about emotional capital, let's first convince ourselves that it exists. Suppose that you buy someone a Rolls Royce. The only catch is, that person is dead. So he won't be showing any excitement towards your gift any time soon. Now suppose he's not dead, just deeply depressed. How much is that Rolls Royce worth to him? What if he already owns three of them? Or what if he simply hates that kind of car? You've just spent how many thousands of money-dollars for a thing whose value could be anywhere from priceless (if it were the person's lifelong dream to own it) all the way down to 0 (for the person who will never be able to reap any benefits from it at all).

And there are stock market panics, sports events and movies into which we funnel our disposable income, parties and leisure costs—including the sneakiest emotional leisure investment of them all: the vacation escape from the lives already available to us. That is, the same trip I'd pay $5000 for might be available to you for $20, the cost of a great time at a new place with an old friend.

Although we attempt to measure many tradable things in monetary capital, our ability to reliably, normatively measure our level of fulfillment with those things remains underdeveloped. We don't have a good way of saying, for example, that a $59 video game is worth 3 weeks of enjoyment to you, but it's worth 1 year of enjoyable game nights and 6 friend experiences to me. Usually, we don't even know the basic indirect *monetary* costs associated with the things we buy. A $59 purchase for you may be $118 purchase for me because I, unlike you, have to buy a second $59 controller to do what I want to do with it. And that's the key: we typically purchase things to satisfy certain wants. The more externally held goods, services, and access you need to fulfill certain wants, the more you'll need money. The lower your need for these things in order to fulfill your wants, the less you'll need money. The currency of emotional capital is fulfillment: your closeness to being completely satisfied in a particular area. The more of such closeness you have, the less extra input you need to make up the difference[4].

While certain things like food, transport-tation, housing, and monthly services are constantly being used up by us—thus warranting money—many other things that we think require money actually do not. They require our own ability to be fulfilled upon their acquisition. Would you rather receive the game in a locked safe (unable to be enjoyed), or the enjoyment that the game would have brought without having the game itself? Emotional capital is your access to fulfillment, whether or not you have purchasable goods and services to sponsor that fulfillment. It is important enough that we've invented drugs to restore our abilities to be fulfilled when we have lost such abilities. We pull our money from the banks en masse when we expect our fulfillment with those banks to plunge.

Although the traditional capital model is built on the idea of resource scarcity, the fulfillment needs of individuals remain with them for as long as they are not dead. We'll keep being hungry again, and we'll keep satiating our appetites again. We'll keep

_____

[4] This is in line with a very interesting contrapositive claim by David Fagundes. See the References section.

wanting some set of experiences which satisfy our psychologies, and we'll keep behaving in those wanted ways for as long as our living personalities remain our own. In this way, though there really will be a limit on the amount of space, the number of bills in circulation, the amount of goods produced by a chain of humans along a limited industrial span, there WILL NOT be a limit on 1) our capacity to want, 2) our capacity to communicate to others, or 3) our capacity to occupy a role in whatever context we're in (unless you're both invisible and immaterial).

If you're alive, interaction-capable, and you have a material form, not only will emotional and other non-monetary forms of capital be available to you, they will also be available in endless supply consummate with your behavioral lifespan. Even if you "lost everything" goods-wise, food and physical protection would be the only things you would absolutely need to keep resupplying in order to continue living stably as a body. The rest of it depends on what the society, species, or environmental conditions train you to expect. This is not to say that caveman living is favorable. It is to say, however, that almost EVERYTHING we think of as purchasable necessity has its roots in socio-emotionally conditioned expectation. We'll need to keep this in mind as we attempt to untangle our emotional capital from our monetary capital.

While monetary capital trades in scarce form-bearing goods, emotional capital trades in lifelong-renewable fulfillment states. This brings us to our first comparison of emotional transfer with money transfer:

> ***Receiving* money is usually better than giving it, unless you have extra.** In general, because you know the goods that satisfy you better than anyone else, it is better for you to receive monetary capital than it is to give it away.

Money in your own hand corresponds to more you-fitting acquisition of the goods you want. If you gave it away, you (typically) couldn't be sure that others would acquire goods on your behalf better than you could. Typically, that is. (There are exceptions to this depending on whether you have a relationship with a "buyer" on your behalf.)

Emotional capital, however, is another story. Unlike monetary capital which is usually better to receive than to give, emotional capital is generally better for you to

EXPAND IN CAPACITY FOR EVERYONE around you than it is to receive or give.

Spreading emotional capital is usually better than hoarding it.

Receiving fulfillment from others without giving it back decreases your emotional value to them. Giving fulfillment to others around you without receiving it back increases the expressive (psychological capital) burden on you, as they transition from being truly fulfilled by you into simply expecting your donation to them as a behavioral role. Where emotional capital is concerned, the richest people are those who fulfill themselves and their interactants equally.

Emotional and monetary capital do have something in common, though. As with monetary capital, free riders hurt proper exchange. If you want to be emotionally rich for the long run, you'll need to curb your interactions with things you can't emotionally sustain.

The next two rules of thumb for emotional capital are as follows:

If it drains you of fulfillment, expect your desire for monetary and psychological "purchases" related to it to increase.

If you drain *it* of fulfillment, expect it to eventually replace you with something more fulfilling.

The reasons for this will become clear as we explore the other two remaining forms of capital.

Money lives in the goods and services you buy. Fulfillment lives in the experiences you think you need. Being money rich is essentially about what you have (for exchange). Being emotionally rich is more about the level of satisfaction that everything around you can hold (for you to feel). I initially began exploring non-capital wealth when I realized how little I cared for capital wealth, given the opportunity to simply write books about things I liked. By investigating things like social status, relationships, asteroids, and economies, I gradually became richer and richer in emotional fulfillment—learning that I didn't actually need to wait for retirement to live out my lifelong dream of being an independent social scientist. That is, if I had a million dollars, I would do exactly what I'm doing now—writing something like this book.

But if I had a million dollars at the time of this writing, (I don't,) I wouldn't have begun investigating this topic in the first place; this particular book, written largely for people are not rich, wouldn't exist. Sometimes, your emotional fulfillment actually requires that you *lack* certain other forms of capital—at least for a time—because the things that genuinely fulfill you become harder and harder to see against the backdrop of all the other measures you think you need.

A person who values his own unique accomplishment may better realize this through a lack of social capital. A person who values genuine support independent of commodifiable status like I do, may better realize this through a lack of money capital. A person who needs to survey and learn openly from the behaviors of others may better realize this through a lack of psychological capital of his own. The basic rule is, if you get your fulfillment from the *quest* for a thing more than you do via the thing itself, you can develop vast emotional wealth more quickly by NOT having that thing. But you'll need to appreciate the opportunity inherent in the quest—your own skills as an experience maker—in order to take advantage of this.

To the extent that our leisure purchases largely comprise a series of trades for fulfillment-sponsoring items, the more accustomed we are to paying for new fulfillment, the harder it may be to find fulfillment in what we already have access to without payment. Having high emotional capital renders the trade of consumable goods less important, so that the role of time as a toll-taker—the urgency in seeking further payment towards the next round of purchases—becomes much lower.

I remind the reader that this isn't a criticism of money, riches, or traditional capital. It's a case for paying attention to *why* we need to buy what we buy. Are the goods we're exchanging as effective in fulfilling us as we expect, or are there more reliable, longer lasting sources of that same kind of fulfillment buried elsewhere in our surrounding relationships to things? Here's one more rule of thumb to wrap up this section:

> If it's an object or a service that you need but are not <u>directly</u> fulfilled by, a fully monetary exchange may be the best way to trade for it. Otherwise,

> if it's an object or service you don't need or something you *are* directly fulfilled by, you

might combine some other form of capital
to trade for it or have someone else get it
for you.

Why someone else? Here we assume that,
ideally, EVERYONE around you shares in your
store of fulfillment, and that at least one
among them would prefer to provide it for you
if they see it as more convenient than letting
you seek it yourself. This is rooted in research
on altruism and bonding which we won't get
into here, but it essentially rests on the idea
that acceptance of our behaviors requires that
we (not surprisingly) do some behaving.
Acceptance of others as fulfilling us requires
that they see themselves as performing
fulfilling acts for us. If you are to be
sustainably emotionally wealthy, your whole
crew—including the environment which feeds
your emotions—needs to be emotionally
wealthy. Barring this, the idea that some actor
isn't pulling their emotional weight will spread
quickly.

Measuring Fulfillment

Because our capacity for fulfillment is, in
most people, continually renewable across our
lifetimes, we really only have three basic levels
of fulfillment for every activity we engage:
enough, not enough, and more than enough.

Using these as a starting point, let's develop a simple scale for determining your fulfillment with any state at any time.

- **Enough**: where you have the amount of a thing required to do what you intend.

- **Not Enough**: where you need more of a thing in order to have the amount required for your intentions.

- **More than Enough**: where you have enough, and even after you have done what you intended, you still have more of the thing left over.

Based on the above you can see that "enough" depends on two factors: 1) the amount of something and 2) what you intend to do with that something. Here we can see why some people seem to never have enough affection, power, or money; if their intention is simply to use affection to get more affection, for example, the intention precludes sufficiency in the amount they have. This would be like saying, "Once I find that love I'll be able to find more love." "It takes money to make money." And so on. When it comes to enough, if the means and the ends are the same, satisfaction will be harder to achieve.

Besides the basic three, there is a second kind of "more than enough" and a second kind of "not enough."

- **More than enough to share/export**: where you have so much more than enough that you must distribute the excess in order to continue doing what you intend.

- **Sub-Not Enough**: where your position of not enough is so great that you must continually seek an external supplier to provide the thing for you.

Let's arrange these five states of fulfillment and give them names.

Vacuum	Need (Demand)	Enough	Extra (Supply)	Source
- ∞	-1	0	1	∞
Sub-not enough	Not enough	Enough	More than enough	More than enough to share

We might ask, *Is this some kind of moral message? When would we ever have so much of something that we are <u>required</u> to share?* Consider a piece of electronics, like a microwave. On the one hand, it requires power and produces heat to do its job. On the other hand, if it produces too much heat it can become dangerous. CPUs, animal bodies, environments, and economic surpluses which signal spending inefficiencies all work the same way. We might dispense with the idea that "more" is always better. Past the limit of stable operation, a system running a pervasive surplus often signals a failure to properly direct its energy/traded unit towards other functions. When you have so much of something that it simply builds up, but lack the proper trading partners to receive the excess from you, you enter the realm of role inefficacy among your surrounding interactants. In the next chapter we'll see how such ongoing super-surpluses in money and emotional capital in particular both lead to decreases in psychological capital: the role you are perceived to play in favor of those whom you would keep around you, or who need what you have. Scrooge McDuck may have enough money to swim in, but as long as he doesn't give back to Duckberg, a scrooge he shall remain.

Super-surpluses, by the way, are the foundation of psychological capital—where unduplicatable, individually-complete skill sets form the ultimate static currency.

Although we speak of having "enough money," money isn't actually measured in terms of "enough;" it's measured in ordinal numbers $1, $2, $3,... Here every dollar earned qualifies you for a slightly higher value purchase, so unlike fulfillment, differences in monetary levels are incrementally meaningful. Whether your purchases on those levels *fulfill* you is a different matter. Fulfillment is counted on a two-way scale negative through positive. What matters is whether you can do what you intend, and how much work you'll need to put in to reach sufficiency in the thing you are to trade.

Having "enough money" in general

only makes sense when comparing amounts to "valuated" amounts. (And that assumes you can't negotiate better prices or different sources, once again challenging whether "enough" really is what we think it is.)

Having "enough money
to live comfortably"

is closer to a statement of emotional security with what can be purchased.

Having "enough fulfillment
with the potential fulfillment
available through the things your
money can purchase"

might be an even more accurate phrase than the generic alternatives above it. Alas, without a list of estimated costs against which to compare our money, the idea of having "enough of it" puts money in the role of a fulfiller: vague, immeasurable, and reductive of our broader emotional aims.

There is something important to note about the five different levels of fulfillment above: None of them is necessarily bad. Vacuums, for example, are one of the major motivators for forming partnerships; the company that brands the water may never have the interest in manufacturing the bottle it comes in. The logical analyst may always require the charismatic spokesperson to convey the former's results. Where we have fulfillment vacuums in certain roles, others have room to trade their surplus fulfillment in that same role for other behaviors we may offer them. Vacuums aren't bad. Where we have a need for something less pronounced than a vacuum, we might buy it from a reliable supplier, trade for it, or communicate its arrival into being. Everybody needs something. Where we need it from sources beyond ourselves, the development of exchange networks is favored.

Building Emotional Capital

Emotional wealth begins with two basic premises:

1. Everything we prefer to do (including fighting and complaining) is something that we can gain fulfillment from.

2. Every experience consistently provided to us (including certain inequities) is something whose fulfillment we can develop a demand for.

That is, we can develop a demand for both positive and negative experiences.

Now you may say, "There's no way I prefer to do the negative things I do, they're just bad habits. And there's no way I'll develop a demand for the bad treatment I often get from certain people." But when we speak of demand here, we're not talking about what you "like." We're talking about what packages your psychology prefers to put together—how your cognition prefers to capture things. If you think of everyone around you as being consistently selfish, selfishness is a package your brain "demands" in order to make sense of what it's seeing. Even if the others aren't actually being selfish, your preferred heuristic would rather hold that selfishness is

something related to their behavior,
demanding this (possibly wrong, but more
predictable) interpretation over a more
ambiguous one. We want what we turn our
actions toward. Our psychologies want what
we turn our sights towards perceiving.

It turns out then, that we're not so much
building emotional capital as we are
unscrambling it. As children we know nothing.
Then we grow, absorbing all kinds of things.
Growing older still, we begin compartmen-
talizing those patterns which fit us best,
meanwhile filtering, rationalizing, ignoring, or
otherwise de-emphasizing everything else that
doesn't fit the frameworks we've grown into.
Where emotional fulfillment is concerned, the
challenge is to approach satisfaction not only
with the frameworks that fit us, but with the
outsourcing of the frameworks that don't fit
us. If you were a company this would be
obvious. Need another company to supply the
screws for your device? Don't punish your
employees for making bad screws; find a
supplier to handle that for you. Does the
search for a job stress you out? Ask someone
who likes looking out to help you.

One thing that is under-discussed in
introductory economics is the notion of
oversupply. When a consumer demands a

good which is supplied by many sources, how does he decide where to obtain it? Here we typically introduce the ideas of market niche, inferior and substitute goods, scarcity of income, and a family of related quantifiable factors. But there are several simpler factors which are much harder to work into our basic decision models of consumer choice: How close is the supplier? How convenient are they to shop at? How familiar is the brand? How likely is it that we can find other goods we want at the same place? How well does the supplier match our own socioeconomic standards? Some hybrid car buyers, for example, may never consider buying a super duty truck. All of these factors add up to the same end result: We choose sources based on a pattern of internal decision making beyond the calculated economic alone. Here again, fulfillment (this time regarding the choice of supplier) constitutes a key factor in economic choice.

Where we defined fulfillment as "the closeness to the amount of a thing needed to satisfy an end," we can consider the difference between the amount had and the amount needed as being something like (invested) energy—as work, consideration, search, communication, or any other behavior—

needed to approach fulfillment. When we buy things with dollars, we also invest behavioral effort in doing so. That additional effort—to the extent that it is painful, enjoyable, or otherwise—adds a behavioral price to the transaction. This isn't "role" behavior, but desired-undesired behavior. So in this book's framework we would consider it emotional. If time is money and money is time, then both time and money can also be thought of as capitalizable energy. Every capital purchase has a fulfillment-level purchase alongside it.

Fulfillment, although not fully capitalizable, presents us with thresholds beyond which differences in the suppliers we seek for our goods no longer matter. Said another way, our level of fulfillment towards the good provides us with a cutoff for the kinds of trouble we're willing to go through in order to get it. When a certain thing we need is oversupplied, we consider the reasonable amount of work we're willing to put in to get it as the cutoff for which supplier we'll choose. This is all pretty technical, but it is directly related to the buildup of emotional capital.

We can think of an emotionally wealthy person as having fulfillment in general oversupply when averaged across his broad life interactions. That is, he is either a broad supplier or a broad source of people's perceived closeness to their goals (according to our scale). Those "people" actually include himself, others, and (in some cases) groups or institutions. So they don't have to be people *per se*. Notice though, that the person's emotional wealth is heavily dependent on goal-nearness both towards AND from those things around him. The closer he is to a supplier or source of this, the less energy his trading partner will require of him and the less they will need from him in order to maintain him as a source without draining him. The satisfaction needs are light across the group and among each other, so that the group members' broad interactional needs are sustainably, easily realizable.

What to Do with Negative Fulfillment

Now here's something interesting. Most trading partners will also be vacuums for something, so that achieving emotional wealth is not as simple as hanging around perfectly happy people. Instead, the emotionally wealthy person is also challenged to take two kinds of non-goals and integrate them into his fulfillment group as well.

- The negative events he attracts

- The areas where he is in perpetual lack.

In other words, emotional wealth requires that your interaction space also supply you with favorable repackagings of the "bad things" your psychology prefers to put together. Emotional wealth also requires that your interaction space provide you with ongoing compensation for the abilities you *don't* have enough of. Here are some examples:

- If you like to ☝ criticize people, your emotionally wealthy state might supply you with a field of analysis to pick apart to your heart's content. Someone else may need to provide the ☝ open acceptance of everything else.

  If you attract people who ✊ bully you, your emotionally wealthy state might establish you as the ✋ right hand of a stressable person you must protect from insecurity.

  ✋ outlet being bullied← ✊ stressed bully

  Stress befits the bully. You serve as the outlet for their self-validation. Negative-psychologically you may be enemies with this type. Positively you and this TYPE of person (not necessarily the actual bully) both work together to behave according to roles that fit you both ✊✋.

🖐 outlet ~~being disturbed~~ ← 🖐 stressed ~~bully~~

Some other pairing or group in your space may need to provide the more 🖐🖐 relaxed dynamic.

- If you 🖐 lack a stable group of supporters, your emotionally wealthy state may put you on the fringe of a particular field. Someone else may need to provide the more publicly 🕸 popular face.

- If you ¢ struggle to make money, your emotionally wealthy state might emphasize the surveying of how you direct your own power towards a perceivable, measurable goal. So your actual specialty may be trading in agreeable-form-defiant or *invaluable* things. Someone else may need to be concerned with $ form-agreeable, value-bearing money.

- If you have a 🔶 violent temper—knowing that it hurts your relationships—your emotionally wealthy state may render you an intense competitor in a certain personality-fitting area, physically or intellectually. Someone else can be the ☯ mellow one.

- If you are susceptible to 🍷 addiction—returning to a certain kind of tool in order to experience an entire alternative reality—your emotionally wealthy state may render you a musician, dancer, artist or some other "tour guide" for dedicating your actions to the reification of such alternative realities. Someone else will need to be 🛠 foreign to such realities, and may rely on you to habitually take them on a journey through your art.

You get the idea. The aim is for us to take our psychologies, our wants—whatever they consist of, good or bad—and frame them as though they have put us closer to, not farther from, some expressive end. The ultimate expressive end will be the sharpened arrangement of traits that make up our psychological capital (discussed in the next chapter). But for now, we'll note that emotional wealth is *not* about mind-numbing happiness 24-7. It's about being close to or past the level of satisfaction needed to attain whatever you're seeking at the moment, be it conversing, driving, or brushing your hair. If you want enough emotional wealth to serve as a source of it for others, you'll need to position yourself such that people can come to you for the purpose of feeling closer to their goals (in whatever your field of specialty is). You don't need to act as a hub for everyone who comes by, but you do need to cultivate an ability to affect people in that shared fulfilling way when the time arrives.

Recap

- Whereas money tends to be best as a thing you yourself get more of, fulfillment tends to be best as a thing your entire interactant space gains more capacity for, shared and easily traded.

- If you gain high levels of fulfillment and the people around you don't, it will generally cost you psychological capital as someone who provides those people with disappointing amounts of whatever satisfaction currency you have. You stingy bastard.

- If others around you gain high levels of fulfillment at your expense, it will also cost you psychological capital, as their satisfaction with you yields to basic expectation. Your emotional gift to them becomes an expected tax on you.

- Fulfillment is the currency of emotional capital. It comes in only five denominations:

- A <u>vacuum</u>-like need to have someone get it for you

- A <u>demand</u> for some place to help you get it yourself

- <u>Enough</u>

- In extra <u>supply</u> for yourself

- *From* you as the <u>source</u> of it for others

- Vacuums aren't bad unless the places you're absorbing from don't want to give it to you.

- Sources aren't necessarily good if they go unreceived by others, reducing your efficacy as a behavioral supplier. In some situations, you may even be an annoyance to them because their lives aren't made to trade in your special behavior, yet you bowl them over with your power for that behavior anyway.

- An emotionally wealthy person broadly perceives himself as being closer to or past whatever amount of means he needs in order to attain whatever end he's seeking. This is MUCH easier to accomplish when those ends are experiential rather than purchase-dependent, since both the means for purchasing things (money) as well as the number and kinds of things available for purchase (goods and services) are typically limited in their supply. Experience and the satisfiability of wants are not so limited.

- The creation of emotional wealth consists of more than easy trades of fulfillment among your interaction space, although that is a key part of it. This kind of wealth also requires that your psychological tendency to "import" negative experiences be reshaped as an export from something in your interaction space which provides you with a positive counterpart for the (formerly) negative—a source of fulfillment.

- To transform a quality you lack into a source of fulfillment, outsource it to someone or something which enjoys supplying that quality. The more you are able to provide emotional capital to them in return, the more likely they are to stay in your interaction space. We talked about this in a previous bullet.

References

The more of such closeness you have   68
Fagundes, D. (2017). Buying happiness: Property, acquisition, and subjective well-being. *William & Mary Law Review, 58*(6), 1851–1931.

in socio-emotionally conditioned expectation   70
Lucey, T. A., & Maxwell, S. A. (2009). Preservice elementary teachers' confidence teaching about money. *Curriculum & Teaching Dialogue, 11*(1/2), 221–237.

is usually better than hoarding it.   72
Wiltermuth, S. S., & Heath, C. (2009). Synchrony and cooperation. *Psychological Science, 20*(1), 1–5.

are those who fulfill...   72
Gallagher, S. K., & Newton, C. (2009). Defining spiritual growth: Congregations, community, and connectedness. *Sociology of Religion, 70*(3), 232–261.

If it drains you of fulfillment...   73
Grigoropoulou / Γρηγοροπούλου, M., Πατσάκη, Α., Κατσάρη, Β., Σαράφης, Π., Μπαμίδης, Π., Βαρακλιώτη, Α., & Δομάγερ, Φ. (2018). Professional burnout among hospital nursing and administrative staff and the tendency of nurses to move to administrative posts / Η επαγγελματική

εξουθένωση νοσηλευτικού και διοικητικού προσωπικού και διερεύνηση της τάσης μεταπήδησης των νοσηλευτών σε διοικητικές θέσεις. *Archives of Hellenic Medicine / Arheia Ellenikes Iatrikes, 35*(5), 633–641.

If you drain it of fulfillment... 73

Guan, H., Zhu, X., & Zhang, P. (2016). Rule-inequality-aversion preference and conditional cooperation in public goods experiments: Economic experiment evidence from China. *Group Decision & Negotiation, 25*(4), 799–825.

Being emotionally rich is more about... 73

Delp, L., Wallace, S. P., Geiger, B. J., & Muntaner, C. (2010). Job stress and job satisfaction: Home care workers in a consumer-directed model of care. *Health Services Research, 45*(4), 922–940.

continually renewable across our lifetimes 76

D'Acci, L. (2013). Hedonic inertia and underground happiness. *Social Indicators Research, 113*(3), 1237.

Chapter 6: Psychological Capital

Psychological capital consists of the set of behavioral resources a person can draw on for performing a task. More precisely, it's the set of things a person can do in a situation which that situation will not supply for itself. That is, few to no other parties should be expected to handle the task at hand. Although surely there are countless others who can do what you do, there is no one who can do it in the way that you do it—with the same attitude, the same pattern of relating, the same intentions for the next steps, in the same place and time. You're it. Uniqueness is the theme here—a quality for which you are the sole supplier and inexhaustible (non-scarce) source. By relying on you to provide a certain behavior, others knowingly or unknowingly sign *themselves* up for the consequences of your approach to that behavior. Their notions of ease or difficulty, convenience, sociability, optimism or expectation, their sense of security with how the behavior is being performed and even their ability to conceive of future options for themselves are all related to how you convey your own traits as you perform your part.

We don't often think of another person at work as being a type of theme music alongside which we ourselves respond to our own roles, but this is a valuable way of thinking when it comes to understanding psychological capital: the area of experience where we trade in behavioral roles.

Typically when we purchase a service rendered by a lawyer, doctor, teacher or other professional, we purchase more than just the actions done to us. We also purchase a filter on what may or may not be known about the situation. We purchase a certain level of courtesy or respect for our own perspective. We purchase assurance that the service will properly meet our needs once completed. We temporarily hold them accountable for the institutions they represent. A bad experience with one doctor may render us skeptical of the next several thereafter. A teacher who can successfully pass their enthusiasm for the subject onto us may encourage us to pursue the entire subject after them.

One of the reasons why the American medical industry is so costly to so many of the people who rely on its services is because the institution itself has largely evolved to accept payment and reputational value from everyone for a minority of the people's troubles. If my ten employees each give up $5 of pay for a medical plan ($50 total) and only two of them file claims for up to $8 each of payment from the insurance company ($16), the insurance company still has $34 of our investment. But the hospitals themselves wanted more than $8 per patient. They sent each patient a bill for the remainder of a $40 charge. One might pay, one might not, but the odds work out in the end. $12 each would have been sufficient for the actual costs of services. Including a $4 deductible, the additional $32 asked of each was simply a professional's tax for services perceived rendered. Here, the insurance company wins, the hospital wins, and the patient, depending on how much of the remaining bill he is able to pay, shoulders the remaining costs. Why? Because it is the patient—not the company or the business—whose psychological perception of the hospital's role is allowed to vary the most. If you know anyone whose $6,000 bill was miraculously reduced to $900 because of hardship, you will have seen this. Our perception of role makes a difference in the value of things. Combined with a cure-all, caring-image pharmaceutical industry, the American medical industry comprises a vast network of expert-roles receiving profits from public and private sources alike, with equipment and knowledge that regular individuals don't have at home. So the industry is able to charge higher prices for the mysterious and wondrous array of resources it has at its disposal—regardless of whether the services it provides the patient could have just as easily been matched by two days in bed.

Role, along with capital generation potential, is one of the heaviest determinants of professional value. Where a person plays a role which may be <u>easily</u> occupied by another, he will typically be paid less. Where he has the potential to attract entire market segments' worth of revenue, he will typically be paid more.

So actors and sports stars make more than teachers and servers, because their roles can attract entire markets. The teacher and server can't typically do this. An interesting aside to all this, however, is that non-unique, non-dangerous roles that pay less are still occupied by people with unique and "permanently losable" arrangements of psychology. Even though we may think of the restaurant server as one among many, the pattern of tips he receives is evidence to the contrary. Clearly the server's combination of traits and behaviors places a unique stamp on a particular collection of patrons' overall experience. He brings his set of performable abilities to the role, whether or not he can employ his most unique skills on the job. In the end, he is just as unique as the professional actor. He might even *become* the professional actor. Perhaps then it's better to say that we're paid for *perceived* roles rather than actual ones. But if that's the case, where does our true psychological capital fit in the economic picture?

Our psychological capital—the pattern of roles we gravitate towards performing well amongst others—determines what fields we easily fit in. It does not determine how much we're paid in that field beyond its minimally accepted base rate. The values held by the paying institution itself, and our ability to meet those values will adjust our pay and promotional opportunities upwards or downwards depending on how well we serve the cultural ends of the institution. Some of those cultural ends are performance-based, others are based on audiences gained, while some might be based on simple looks. Along these lines, there is some additional news associated with this particular kind of capital:

Because psychological capital trades in roles, it also trades in assumptions about the people applying for those roles. Your looks, body build, sex, temperament, speech patterns, and dress are all a part of your <u>psychological</u> capital (from your perspective; social capital from others' perspectives), as they complete the package you carry from place to place in the performance of your role. A great basketball player who is 5'9" will have a harder time performing his role in the NBA. In the very broad context of economics framed in this book, his height is part of his psychological capital set which influences where he is *allowed* to use his skills. Truly, societies have expectations for what kinds of people belong in certain kinds of places, such that those who don't match these expectations tend to face a society-wide inertia pushing them to perform their roles in some other place. In this way, although you can generally be whatever you want to be in places like the US, you can't always be those things *where* you want to be. So how do you successfully land that niche position which fits you best?

We can't answer that yet. Before discussing niches, we need to develop a measure for role as the currency of psychological capital.

Measuring Psychological Capital

Like money, role ability starts at 0 and counts upwards. Unlike money, role has an

upper limit. There's no such thing as a more-
doctor. Thus we can measure a role using six
basic levels:

   0% (F-0) No skill

  20% (F-2) Learning the skill

  40% (F-4) Practicing the skill

  60% (D)   Using the skill

  80% (B)   Teaching the skill

100% (A+) Inventing on top of the skill

We can just give ourselves a grade for each
area we are fairly skilled in. We can also think
in terms of percentiles. If you believe you can
outperform every person in a group of 199,
you would be in the 199/200th or 99.5% level.
Along these lines, consider that your ability to
use the role's skill (D level) is enough to get
you considered for a job that required that
skill.

In order to assemble a niche, we'll need to
put together three areas where we rate
ourselves at an A+ level. This isn't necessarily
about outperforming everyone or even being
confident in our abilities. It's really about that
thing which WE ALONE do among our peers.
Making people laugh, organizing better than
most, convincing people, and so on. This is a

thing which others might come to us specifically for, and not just because it's our job title. Once we've identified this, we need to add at least two more things: how we execute that role, and what we do with the results of our success, moving onto the next task. Together these form a complete picture of our A+ niche:

- The role

- The process and outlook for performing it

- The handling of its results

And that's it. The construction of a niche. This is the skill pattern which, if you could turn every task into one that requires this approach, you would never tire of performing it. Consider this to be your sole unit of psychological "money"—your expressive equivalent of a dollar. In jobs you perform, you lend your employers different versions of this psychological role in exchange for a moneyed-paycheck. In your normal relationships, when people need your help, they come to you for the personal version of this same thing. Ideally.

If someone put you into a machine and passed around your behavioral effects on others as money, what kinds of people would "spend" you? What kinds of things would you be useful for buying? Knowing your best role pattern is only the first part of building psychological wealth. The second part consists of turning all roles you perform into this one.

In the previous chapter we talked about how too much (super-surplus) monetary and emotional capital can sometimes lead to a drop in psychological capital. While having lots of money and lots of happiness can certainly make you feel good psychologically, having so much money that you know you're not helping the external causes you actually value, having so much happiness that the people around you are unhappy by comparison—these are reflections of you as an actor in the world you occupy. The more you get without affecting that world in a useful way, the less useful you are to those who still live in that world you've withheld from. In terms of psychological capital, your behavioral niche would be largely unspent here. Thus the key to psychological wealth is the reverse of that belonging to monetary wealth:

With money it's better to receive.

With emotions it's better to share.

With psychology it's better to spend.

The A+ niche you personally occupy is already yours in unending supply until the day you die; making yourself useful is the basis of role efficacy. For every person who hates their job and can't wait to retire from it, there's a high chance that the same person does not get the level of psychological capital needed from that job to bring them contentment with it. If they're not supplementing that job with something they are role-effective in, then finding a "better" job, retiring, or even winning the lottery may not bring the contentment they need. These would change the social, socioemotional, and monetary contexts respectively, but When it comes to psychological capital, more money or less work aren't the thing. More love for the work with *less of a concern for the money* is exactly the thing. You hope to find the outlet from which you'll <u>never</u> want to retire.

The psychologically wealthy person is effective in any role you put him in. That is, any role is his role, where his personal currency is always accepted. But this isn't about fitting in everywhere. Instead it's about developing an overall outlook for how (or why) you do things, then focusing on the places that need you. The outlook, when added to your niche, is your sense of purpose—your brand—which allows you to see every role you perform as contributing to the bigger agenda you've chosen.

Psychological wealth is all about knowing you have what it takes, wherever you land. You might be surprised, however, to find that this is not the same as any of the following:

- Being an extrovert

- Thinking you can master everything

- Being confident (or overconfident)

- Knowing how to do the exact thing you've been asked to do

Although these qualities can help, a person can still have psychological wealth without them. Instead, the real keys to building psychological wealth are these:

- Knowing that, whatever skills you do bring to the task, you will reasonably adapt them to fit the goal

- Being able to recognize when you've tried your best, beyond which no person or system can tell you otherwise

Fitting what you bring to match the needs of the system you are in as well as recognizing and operating at your maximum are two of the most important routes to seeing every role you play as one being played at its peak. Perhaps you can see how this kind of "effective integration" can be more useful and more beneficial than niche-specific mastery for your sense of being great anywhere. Specific task requirements change, the need to change with that change doesn't.

Building Psychological Capital

The simplest route to building psychological capital can be found through an easy trick: We'll call it the **Two Obsessive Hobbies** trick

1) <u>Take a thing you love to actively *do*</u>, whether or not you're paid, whether or not anyone tells you to, whether or not anyone else is around. Watching TV doesn't count. It needs to be an active behavior coming from you yourself rather than one sent to you. Something like a service you could provide.

2) <u>Recall a thing you *used to* actively do</u>, especially prior to high school (before the social pressures began to set in, crowding out old notions of youthful fun).

3) <u>Find the common ground between these two activities</u>. Voila. 10,000 hours of whatever that is, for many of us already logged.

After childhood years spent building Lego and Sim Cities, and adult years smashing data together with colored squares, I found for example that I was a "system structurer." I'm not a writer, but if I'm putting together a system, a book can get produced. I'm not a teacher, but if I'm explaining a social situation to people, teaching can happen. I'm not a statistician or an astrologer, but if I'm tasked with using certain methods to clarify others' observations or patterns describing those others, statistics can arise—even statistics on a "pseudoscience." In whatever capacity you need me, I will attempt to enter it as a system structurer, and I believe I will be good at it. This is psychological capital.

If you're heavily obsessed with it now and always have been, chances are it is a niche for you.

1. Determining the Role

And now for the fun part. What do you love to actively do, paid or not, told or not, shared company or not? NO EXCUSES! That is, you can't say "I would make beautiful sculptures **if** only I had the time." If you don't have the time and therefore *don't* do it, you *can't* list it. It must be a thing you *do* do. Messaging friends? Criticizing enemies? Picking out outfits? Slaying bosses in MMORPGs? Actively imagining as you read books? **What do you actively do that engages you without cease?** Not what you *would* do. What you *do* do.

When you were young, where did you spend all of your active, voluntary time? What did you like to do non-stop? If your answer is "playing with friends," playing at what? Riding your bike? Okay. Depending on what your answer to the previous question was, you may or may not specify *how* and *where* you liked to ride. Just in case X-games isn't an option for you now. Riding through the neighborhood with friends back then may correspond to active team projects now. Be as specific or as general as you need in order to see the parallels with the previous answer.

Although you don't have to force the answers above to reveal a niche, chances are you will have *something* that constitutes that behavior pattern that you not only love to do, but which your history has allowed you to do to your heart's content. Imagine taking that niche with you as the basis for your attitude towards any situation you're put in. It's powerful. The psychological capital is yours to claim.

2. Determining the Process

The process for exercising your niche will likely be automatic, so there is less of a need to describe this. You'll simply do what you do. Furthermore, going without a description for how you exercise your niche may afford you the open flexibility required of any expert. You're just a good and dedicated team player, critic, artist, analyst, advertiser, people connector, etc... Who needs a blueprint? But there is one component of your process which it truly does help to know: What kinds of conditions can <u>stop</u> you in your niche?

It wasn't until recently that I learned that either [being commanded] or [being compelled to take others' input] could both stop my niche as a system structurer. My systems are my art, and are just as resistant to forcing as you would expect art to be. You discover "stops" by observing those occasions where, in the middle of you're A+ performance you say to the other person, "alright, then do it yourself then."

What kinds of events can cause you to stop your niche work even as people around you basically want you to keep doing it? Imagine those times where you were doing exactly what you loved and specialized in, until someone came along looking to hang around you (and/or your team), only to ruin your work. What is it that they did?

Ideally, environments that minimize the "niche stopper" are the environments you will gradually learn to insist on as you grow in psychological capital. Many readers who may have a hard time identifying their niche up to now might have had that hard time because they have *always* been under their niche stopper. With the understanding that we all have work and family responsibilities that we still have to answer to, try to clear that stuff out as best you can. Cheerful givers make better niche performers.

3. Determining the Handling

What do you do with the results of your niche? Another reason you might have had a harder time identifying your source of psychological capital might be because it's been a long time since you did anything with the results of your psychological capital. After a while in building my Lego buildings, I decided never to tear them down. My results had to be permanent. Now, my data and scholarly structures have to be permanent as well, immortalized in book form. If I'm not writing or recording my findings in a "forever format," my exercise of psychological capital is incomplete. In situations where you're allowed to exercise your niche, but not allowed to reap the results you want, the question becomes, "Why bother?"

You can assess the results of niche performance by looking at the things that you are most proud of in light of the completion of that performance. For me it's a finished building, book, or data workflow, whether or not anyone sees it. (With many skills, doing it without external rewards is how you really know it's part of your psychological capital.)

In light of the completion of your psychological specialty, what kinds of results are you most proud of?

The above three sections combined will form the basis of your psychological capital. Your ability to take that pattern of thinking and translate it into any role you're given forms the basis of your psychological riches. To surround yourself with people and environments who ask this of you, towards whom you are willing to give it ceaselessly (without overburdening yourself) is the basis of great psychological *wealth*. The aim is to take this pattern of offerings that only you can provide and carry it as your tool of choice anywhere and everywhere you go, making you useful in service to everyone. The confidence that comes with this can be great. The more you give this talent of yours to others, the more you'll receive other forms of capital in return.

Recap

- Psychological capital consists of the combination of behavioral resources which are more or less unique to you. It has roots in your childhood as well as your present, and can be more easily clarified by looking at the patterns of behavior you've been fixated on across these two areas. Not the specific acts. The *patterns of behavior* spanning across those acts.

- A person is compensated for his psychological capital based on his perceived fitness for a role in the eyes of others. Some of this has to do with looks, mannerisms, sex, and other overt factors, such that people looking to apply their skills in one area may find themselves socially "encouraged" into another. It's not always fair, but it doesn't have to affect your assessment of your own psychological capital within. Even if you're put in a social role you didn't plan, a truly psychologically wealthy person can feel right at home with his role efficacy anywhere.

- Psychological capital can be measured via a basic six-level A-F scale. This will reflect the level of mastery in a particular area. The goal is to find areas in which you get an A.

- Psychological capital is not about your ability to do everything or know everything. Instead, it revolves around your ability to turn any situation into one you know how to tackle using your own unique way of tackling things generically at your best.

- You can determine your behavioral niche by combining your present, unrewarded fixation with your major childhood unrewarded fixation.

- It's not necessary to define the details of your niche process, but it is useful to identify the kinds of things that knock you out of niche performance, so that you can minimize these factors wherever you can.

- Your handling of the results of your niche performance is important in that, without results, the chances of your valuing your own niche performance may be lower. It will be much more difficult to build up psychological capital if you don't have a valuable result attached to its use.

References

behavioral resources a person can draw on   95

Luthans, F., Youssef-Morgan, C. M., & Avolio, B. (2007). *Psychological capital: Developing the human competitive edge.* Oxford University Press.

a vast network of expert-roles   97

Embrett, M., & Randall, G. E. (2018). Physician perspectives on Choosing Wisely Canada as an approach to reduce unnecessary medical care: a qualitative study. *Health Research Policy & Systems, 16*(1).

which WE ALONE do   101

Littman-Ovadia, H., Lavy, S., & Boiman-Meshita, M. (2017). When theory and research collide: Examining correlates of signature strengths use at work. *Journal of Happiness Studies, 18*(2), 527–548.

that you would never tire of performing   102

O'Brien, M. K., & Ahmed, A. A. (2019). Asymmetric valuation of gains and losses in effort-based decision making. *PLoS ONE, 14*(10), 1–21.

Chapter 7: Social Capital

There are already many definitions of social capital, but for this book's economic purposes we will introduce one more. Social capital consists of the psychological, emotional, or monetary capital which other people or groups are willing to share with you as a result of your relationship with them. The strength of social capital is that it potentially provides every other resource that you yourself lack or have difficulty obtaining on your own. Before we go further in discussing this form of capital, let us emphasize one major point:

If it's not psychological capital that you can give inexhaustibly,

if you don't have the monetary capital to trade for it, don't want to trade monetary capital for it, can't measure it, point to it, or agree on its value or form,

if it's not a direct product of the emotional capital that follows you yourself wherever you go, *you will likely need to get it through social capital* (that is, if you want it).

Social trading is useful for outsourcing certain experiences which just aren't as easy for you to initiate on your own.

One major byproduct of social capital (which most of us rely on without knowing it) may actually surprise you: it's monetary capital. And you get it from your social relationship with your job. Surprising isn't it? It turns out that most of us who need to work for a living do not actually have enough monetary capital to live the kinds of lives we want, so we set up social relationships with our places of work in exchange for a monetary paycheck. The job "likes" what we do, so it gives us monetary capital in exchange for the mostly social, sometimes psychological capital we provide to it alongside our colleagues. By pooling our mostly social/ideally psychological capital with those of others, the business can then produce a product or service worth far more than our individual efforts monetarily. It issues this product or service out to the public in order to bring in higher traditional capital returns, while the product itself acts as an enabler of mainly emotional or psychological fulfillment among the consumers within that public.

Remember earlier when we said that a trade naturally involves two kinds of capital? Here we see the full array of components in the circular flow model. It isn't as simple or mechanical as a business trading a paycheck for "labor" and goods for revenue. The paycheck is monetary, the labor is social and psychological (sustained by a tolerable emotional environment), the goods fulfill a primarily emotional or psychological need (social if it's more leisure or high-brand related), and the revenue is monetary again. In this chain, social capital is a measure of the connection strength between one actor's chain of transfer and another's. Low social capital limits us to our own transactional worlds. High social capital allows us to access some parts of the transactional worlds of others.

How Much of the Other Capital Types Do You Get from a Social Relationship?

Most social capital connects us to other social capital, a decent amount of other's psychological capital, some of their emotional capital, and less of their monetary capital. The rule is, the more ubiquitous (or freely obtainable) the capital type, the more likely you are to get it from a social exchange. Let's look at a very rough estimate of some likelihoods you might encounter.

Potential social relationships are truly everywhere: If you had **10 actors**, for example, you would have **90** one-way relationships among them (10 Actor A's x 9 Actor B's) **or** **45** potential binary relationships among them (10 x 9 / 2).

Every person may be considered to have a niche they might be willing to donate: 10 actors, **10 niches**.

Some people can afford emotionally rich sharing while many can't: 10 actors, **5 emotional donators** (if it's 50% likely one will give to you or take from you.

And because monetary capital really is scarce, you might have only **1** "richest person of all" who *needs* to give his money to something in order to be psychologically whole. Expect fewer of these than the number of emotional donors since the capital supplier also needs to be emotionally fulfilled in doing so.

Accordingly, we'll guess that for every 10 actors, half of which get fulfillment from giving, you might get very lucky and have **1** capital donor. If you're lucky.

The above estimates aren't real numbers, mind you. They're just a super rough sketch of the likelihood that you'll receive certain kinds of capital from your social lottery. No, not every social relationship will lead to money for you, but it will almost always lead to some combination of other social relationships or other psychological resources—the kinds of capital to which we're all granted default access to at least one unit. Rarer forms like emotional fulfillment and monetary value will require richer social relations than the norm, and this leads us to a discussion of how social capital is measured.

Measuring Social Capital

There is a formal research field called social network analysis which takes a technical, quantitative approach to social networks. SNA, as it is called, employs various specialized statistical methods, fields such as graph theory which most of us don't see unless we majored in it in college, and certain fancy software for looking at people's relationships in correlation. Instead of getting into all of that, we'll take a more basic approach to measuring your social capital which uses a simple 0-5 scale for what you think you're getting and giving from your various relationships.

Now before we go rating your relationships, let's address one major problem with the assumptions of something like social network analysis: Although we do it with large data sets, real humans can't just rate their friends using a single unified standard. Any of us who have a friend Joe who would get on our nerves *but for* our other friend Jane, knows that having one person meet certain needs changes the kinds of needs you expect different other people to meet. In a typical marriage, you don't expect people other than your spouse to meet the spouse standard, so that's a kind of rating that belongs only to one person. That's how we work in real life. We don't actually rate 10 people on "warmth." We assess the overall warmth of our (immediate) network, where your two warm friends are really warm and your two jerk friends aren't warm at all. But they're still okay in your book. Accordingly, we'll rate social capital using one of the simplest methods around: by estimating your *overall* social satisfaction.

Rate your overall satisfaction with the following forms of capital from 0-5. (For the questions below "main support group" refers to the people who most heavily influence where you're at and where you're going in life. It could include friends, bosses, enemies, etc.)

	Very Dissatisfied					Very Satisfied
	0	1	2	3	4	5
From you to Others						
Monetary: Overall Satisfaction with your economic situation						
Psychological: Overall satisfaction with your performance of skills; how good you are in what you do across most situations						
Social: How good or valuable a person you are to most people you have access to (not just friends, but colleagues and others)						
Emotional: How satisfied you are with your outlook and display of emotions towards others; how easy it is for you to express to your satisfaction						
From Others to You						
Monetary: Overall satisfaction with the social-economic tier of your main support group; the kinds of experiences they can help you have						
Psychological: Overall satisfaction with the "expert" or "good at what they do" level of your main support group						
Social: Overall satisfaction with the span and quality of relationships you can call on for whatever you need;						
Emotional: Overall satisfaction with the way your main support group members express their wants or preferences towards you						

It's not actually meaningful to add up the above, though if you did put all 5s or all 0s it would definitely say something. More interesting to note are those areas which you might not have rated as expected. These have everything to do with how the questions were asked, but the questions were asked in ways that separated the capital forms. For example, I thought sure I would have rated my monetary satisfaction items lower, but it turns out my craving for a million dollar lifestyle and million dollar friends was actually more of a desire for less emotional suppression—from others as seen by me. (I rated this a 1.5). As we learned in the riches-dreaming exercise earlier in the book, so much of what we think we want to purchase actually consists of what we want to simply happen—purchased or not. The above table can help you see which of the capital forms you really might work on. Sometimes it's monetary receipt, sometimes it's monetary spending. But not always.

Now why would we have dumped all four capital forms under social capital? We did so because most of our capital lives are actually outsourced. The mortgage company owns our house. That guy you know hosts the wicked parties. That A+ niche you have is only A+ because your clients say so. Overall, the two-capital nature of trade in almost any situation means that your money is no good without stores, friends, family and other relationships to spend it on. Even if you only want it for security, your money is no good without emotional safety to pile it towards. And of course you get no money but for the others who gave it to you—whether inherited, paycheck-based, or client-paid. Scattered across your social networks are people with whom you trade all four forms of capital, though at this point we've gotten used to thinking of capital more as consisting more of generic tradable units than it consists of simply dollars. Not all transactions involve money, but they almost always involve relationships set up for trade.

A Note on Building Social Capital

We can't actually outline specific steps for building social capital because, like psychological capital, everyone's preferences are different. As an introvert, I used to hear extroverts tell me all the time "You just have to get out there." "Taking the first step can be hard." "You just have to be yourself." The assumption here is that making new connections is desirable, and that may be. But even if it is, some people fare better by letting the greatest connections come to them. Some people find that their current connections are the only ones who understand them or are worth trusting. Other people only care about making connections that involve their work or their art or something similar. For these people, building social capital will be a function of where they actually get value out of the relationships they form, where "going out there" and making their network newer and larger may actually dilute their fulfillment instead.

So what's the best advice for building social capital? I'd recommend building your psychological capital. Money may buy bodies near you, but not necessarily the relationships you want. Emotional fulfillment can keep a network strong if you share it, but you need parties to share it with. Remember, though, how it was better to give psychological capital than to receive? Development of your A+ niche makes it easier for you to give something willingly and near inexhaustibly, and affects the attitude you bring to your associations. It's the attitude that counts, not necessarily the action. The more confident you are in what you uniquely bring to the table, the less likely you are to feel that not enough others are bringing it for you.

Protect Ya Net

We never mentioned how social capital should be moved around. If it's better to receive money than to give it, better to give efficacy than to not give it, and better to share fulfillment than to stockpile it, how should we handle social capital?

It's better to *selectively spend* your social capital. Share access to your network, but only when doing so enriches the network. And yes, hooking up an outsider CAN enrich the network by adding the outsider to it. That's how networks are built in the first place. Hooking up outsiders is also one of the best ways to make new allies of former enemies. Being greedy with your social capital will only rob you of new experiences, *but...*

One major issue in our current society stems from our way of plugging into too many things. Plugging our friends into too many side quests. Squirrelin' out. When you plug your network mates into outlets that don't build them our you, you run the risk of dropping your social capital. One example that comes to mind for me is in the spreading of bad news. Lee isn't really in my network, and has offended me. I tell Jean. Then I introduce Jean to Lee for whatever reason, plugging her

in. Jean takes my biases with her. Now both
of our relationship with Lee is worse. This
happens ALL THE TIME when our social
capital spreads its members' problems
around. Your social capital is there as a
resource for you and you for them. Others can
play too. But beware the tendency to invest
your social capital in things that *drop* your
fulfillment. Not surprisingly, you may risk
dropping the quality of your outlook, despite
the good intentions of the network overall. But
your network won't be able to fix it. You'll
have to.

Recap

- Social capital measures your access to
  various kinds of resources via parties
  besides yourself. Far from a state of
  weakness or insufficiency, social capital is
  the engine which powers basic trade
  among parties and the basic formation of
  markets at all. Directly related to the more
  formal economic concept of competitive
  advantage, your emotional, psychological,
  social, and monetary strengths constitute
  the services you bring to others who will,
  in turn, provide resources to you which
  you are less efficient in gathering. You may
  even be a vacuum for those resources.
  Combining with the right social partners,

however, can turn your vacuum or your oversupply into a key ingredient for a much more prosperous collective effort. You just need to be ready to get past yourself, and get over the oft-celebrated notion that more is always better, before you can really trade successfully.

- You build social capital by building psychological capital; for some this will involve getting out there, but for others it won't. It depends on where the person actually finds value in their relationships. Get good at giving something of yourself— your A+ niche *outlook* (also known as being good at being yourself)—and you'll find that the people you attract will more likely be people who want to be there, not just people who are paid to be there.

- Psychological capital is meant to be given out (as long as you don't let others exploit you). Social capital is meant to be intentionally invested. There are countless ways to distract your main support group by plugging its members into an ocean of unfulfilling events, so that it becomes important to sustain your social capital with inputs that enrich it. Take that however you want. Your main support group needs good trade with *you*, not bad trade with problem sources. If you have a main support group, when was the last time you helped reinforce their unique value to you? This will be important when we talk about micro collectives later on.

References

is useful for outsourcing 118

Liping Qian, Pianpian Yang, & Jiaqi Xue. (2018). Hindering or enabling structural social capital to enhance buyer performance? The role of relational social capital at two levels in China. *Journal of Business-to-Business Marketing, 25*(3), 213–231.

social network analysis 121

Buch, H. H. (2014). Social network analysis and critical realism. *Journal for the Theory of Social Behaviour, 44*(3), 306–325.

using a single unified standard 122

Kwak, D., & Kim, W. (2017). Understanding the process of social network evolution: Online-offline integrated analysis of social tie formation. *PLoS ONE, 12*(5), 1–16.

are actually outsourced 124

Smith, M. M. (2008). Lifestyle analysis: Guide to an accurate and defensible net worth statement. *American Journal of Family Law, 22*(3), 124–127.

almost always involve...set up for trade 125
Tovar Jalles, J., & Tavares, J. (2015). Trade, scale or social capital? Technological progress in poor and rich countries. *Journal of International Trade & Economic Development, 24*(6), 767–808.

attitude that counts, not necessarily the action. 126
Taghian, M., D'Souza, C., & Polonsky, M. (2012). A study of older Australians' volunteering and quality of life: Empirical evidence and policy implications. *Journal of Nonprofit & Public Sector Marketing, 24*(2), 101–122.

you run the risk of dropping your social capital 127
Brockman, B. K., Park, J. E., & Morgan, R. M. (2017). The role of buyer trust in outsourced CRM: Its influence on organizational learning and performance. *Journal of Business-to-Business Marketing, 24*(3), 201–219.

basic trade among parties and... 128
Knack, S., & P. Keefer. (1997). Does social capital have an economic payoff? A cross-country investigation. *The Quarterly Journal of Economics, 112*(4), 125–188.

with inputs that enrich it 129

Molony, T. (2009). Carving a niche: ICT, social capital, and trust in the shift from personal to impersonal trading in Tanzania. *Information Technology for Development, 15*(4), 283–301.

Chapter 8: Who Will Trade with Me?

While writing this book I came to a realization. In the handful of areas where I wanted to build a particular kind of capital, I knew where I needed to go for trading, but couldn't or wouldn't go there. You may know that teaching others (psychologically and socially) is a good way for you to fill in a particular hole in your emotional capital, but won't do it because you feel you must make monetary capital to pay the bills. But you've been making monetary capital and the emotional hole is still there. What do you do? Do you just resign yourself to slavedom? There has to be a way to do the thing you want without passing through the thing you don't want. We know this because your psychology seems to have no trouble drawing this straight line. It's all the external events you observe in between here and there which make that straight line crooked before you can stay on the line long enough to see it through in the practical world.

So how do we pull in the types of trading partners we've identified for filling in our capital deficits? We know they're out there. We may even talk to them every day, but without a strong enough social relationship to ask them for what we want. In the absence of psychic powers we do what most successful businesses do: We advertise.

Here's what I offer to EVERYONE (capital type X).

I remind you that I offer it to you (capital type X).

Here is the (brand) culture I like to get from EVERYONE LIKE YOU (capital type Y).

You don't have to trade with me, but if you do, here is the currency you can give me which helps me trade with you even more (capital type Z).

All that said, what can I do for you (capital type Q)?

Broadly,

- **Capital type X will be whichever of the eight capital areas (four *from* you, four *to* you) you are inexhaustibly good at offering,** even if it is a vacuum, even if it is actually a them-to-you extraction. It doesn't matter what it is, to or from whom. If it happens everywhere you go, no matter who you're interacting with, consider it your prime offering.

- **Capital type Y is the hole you're trying to fill in your capital space**, whether you're looking to get more money, give more money, be more effective psychologically, or receive more effective people socially. Again, it doesn't matter what it is. If you want this kind of resource, you want it. Depending on the quality of the relationship you're doing this in, you may or may not ask *the other* to provide it. You just need to let them know it's what you like in general. If it isn't on their radar, don't expect them to read your mind.

- **Capital type Z** is actually not about you. **It is the thing you've determined that it fulfills the other person to give to you** (or to everyone). Enable the kinds of resources they like "exporting" inexhaustibly, and they may get more out of giving to you.

In our consumer market, we actually *love* giving out money to businesses. Not because we "really" love it, but because we're trained to think ourselves obligated to make these kinds of trades. We work jobs we hate so that such trades can be made. We pressure and (de)value ourselves in terms of the number and amount of such trades our income allows us to make. So if I'm a business, my aim is to convince you that you can give me more of your money in exchange for some quality experience you want. The rest rides on your socialization into this as a fair and desirable arrangement. Is it? Probably. Until you come to see non-capital trades as also having value, monetary-capital trades will be some of the most enticing of all to you. So it's easy to make large numbers of people feel fulfilled through the money they've given to me in exchange for whatever I've sold them. I just need to make sure that whatever it is meets their current (often non-(monetary) capital) needs.

o In relationships though, monetary capital isn't normally the thing people want to give to you. Psychological efficacy is. But even that will vary with yours and the other's specific situation.

- **Capital type Q is the all-important current hole in the *other* person's capital space.** You won't normally know what this is. They won't know either. Most of us are trained to think it's money. We're also trained to stay out of other people's money-related affairs. So we end up facing this problem of the other party's personal worth. If only there were thought bubbles which let us say to the other,

> "Just show me the deficit you
> want to fill and the niche you
> use in spite of it. You know you
> want to."

> "I'll give you the surplus capital
> I'm oversupplied in for that
> deficit. It will make me feel more
> effective in my filling my deficit."

But how do you propose this without breaking and entering into someone's self-valuation? Just advertise. "I have surpluses for sale if you know anyone." Some people would call this manipulation. But as is the case in sales, It's not manipulation if you truly believe in your product, and want to tell your client about it without kicking in their door.

That's all there is to it. Ultimately, if you want to receive something, the giver needs to have some reason for giving it to you. Sometimes those reasons are internal to them (good feels), sometimes those reasons are external (cash payment). Although it is not necessarily the case that you need to give in order to receive, it is usually the case that your giver needs to receive *something from somewhere* in order to give to you, lest they get drained by everyone else who asks for that thing they're so good at giving. Do everyone one a favor. Be mindful of the giver's need to recharge. Unless you happen to meet them on their yacht, kicking their feet up without a care, chances are they want or need something that you could help contribute to. If you go into the potential trade with Capital types Z and Q (their niche and their deficit) on your brain, it will be easier to form a sustainable non-monetary market with them.

Trades are much easier to enter when you consider both sides of the exchange.

A Practical Puzzle

To help you identify your psychologically-favored trades, try using the grid below. Put a check mark in any box which strikes you as a kind of trade which commonly happens, or which you commonly observe in your life. The trade can be actual or abstract, just make sure it happens <u>for you</u>. If it doesn't happen for you but you want it to, don't check it. If it doesn't happen for you, but you think it should, don't check it. It has to happen. Your niche market in the chapters to come will be built on trades that actually happen. Leave everything else blank.

If you're really good at a particular kind of trade, you might put two check marks instead of one.

(I'll warn you beforehand, this table is CHALLENGING to fill out. Even after I made it, it was challenging for me. The problem is, we're so used to trading in "things" that we may find it harder to see where we trade in *processes*. Take your time and think about this one, and if it's too abstract, come back to it later. Should you decide to go the route we'll discuss over the next two chapters, you'll be glad you did. It may help to start with the trades which are most obvious to you. I numbered mine from 1st, 2nd, 3rd...)

	In exchange for giving this...	Monetary Capital				Emotional Capital	
I receive this...		Money or Credit	Land	Workers	Objects	Fulfillment inside	Satisfaction with the Outside
Monetary Capital	Money or Credit						
	Land						
	Workers						
	Objects						
Emotional Capital	Fulfillment Inside						
	Satisfaction with the Outside						
Psychological Capital	Effectiveness everywhere						
	Effectiveness in my niche						
	Other people's niche expertise						
	Training in tools that build my niche						
Social Capital	Relationships that help me towards the outside						
	Relationships that defend me from the outside						
	Relationships that challenge me/grow me/clarify me inside						
	Relationships that remind me/defend my existing inside						

Psychological Capital				Social Capital			
Effectiveness everywhere	Effectiveness in my niche	Other people's niche expertise	Training in tools that build my niche	Relationships that help me towards the outside	Relationships that defend me from the outside	Relationships that challenge me/grow me/clarify me on the inside	Relationships that remind me/defend my existing inside

References

their current (often non-(monetary)...) needs 136

Coelho, G. L. de H., Hanel, P. H. P., Johansen, M. K., Maio, G. R., & Back, M. (2019). Mapping the structure of human values through conceptual representations. *European Journal of Personality, 33*(1), 34–51.

Chapter 9: Valuation

How do you determine the market value of something? Typically in a capitalist system, we let the market itself decide, because the capital market already has the largest possible space of non-capital factors built into its trading universe. There are certainly ways to measure the non-capital aspects of these factors, and we've begun to outline ways to assign numbers to such factors throughout this book. But macroeconomics isn't really this book's focus. Instead, we'll assume that a $250,000 house is so priced because the market knew what it was doing. But what about your personal market? Just because houses A and B are both $250,000, doesn't make them equal to you. Security (emotional), neighborhood quality (social, emotional, and psychological), tax rate and house quality (indirect monetary) all contribute to the cost of the houses you're looking at. And so it is with all purchases. There are other costs besides the direct monetary. Whether and how we consider those costs forms the substance of our approaches to the valuation of things.

Back in our discussion of social capital, we rated our eight measures from 0 to 5. The aim of this chapter is not so much to introduce any complex formulas for turning ratings into value. Instead, we will only discuss the broad approach to determining whether something we think should be major is actually "worth it."

Why Are We Doing This?

A good portion of our lives as monetary capital consumers revolves around the quest to make big purchases using years of hard work. We might purchase a retirement from work life for $200,000, a dream house for $450,000, a university education for $90,000. Perhaps these will still be worth the investment five years after they are purchased. Perhaps they won't be. Maybe we will have become so used to them that they will have lost their magic by then. Maybe they will have been the gift that keeps on giving.

Other kinds of purchases are not so simple to quantify. Do you pursue that person's affection or not? Do you visit that hobby group or not? Granted, these aren't so much monetary purchases as they are energy and effort investments, yet these non-capital decisions have an uncanny way of affecting our capital lives. They have consequences for domestic arrangements, friendship, time and activities, the cost or possibility for raising a family, and a whole host of other consequences—not least of which is that grand tower called "social expectation."

If our monetary purchases go towards fulfillment and efficacy-based returns, then fulfillment and efficacy will be good things to consider before we enter major agreements with far reaching consequences. If I really do plan to purchase that house that promises to put me on the financial edge, I need to know why. Is it really because my family *needs* more (psychological or monetary) space, or is it because my spouse and I *want* more (social and emotional) status? Even if we do plan to purchase no matter what, certain decisions are too expensive to base on the wrong expectations. If those decisions are going to cost us, we should at least enjoy what we're paying for.

By investigating how we assign value to things, we ensure that the intangible aspects of our time, energy, and monetary investments get just as much consideration as the tangibles intended to enable those very abstractions. We're buying the material house for the purposes of immaterial enjoyment.

Surely such enjoyment should form a part of our calculations in the first place.

The Time-Energy Value of Money

In economics we often hear about TVM: the time value of money.

- Money and time are related.

- Less money now is preferable to more money later

- Riskier investments should, if successful, pay more

- Time lost is money lost.

These principles hold broadly in an economic system, all other things such as market volatility, trade conditions, convenience to the consumer, producer expertise, consumer knowledge of options, and investor confidence being held constant. But market volatility, consumer convenience, and other such factors indicate to us that there is *much* more at work in a capital system than simply time and money. Namely, the amount of energy or effort required for such conditions to simulate constancy also needs to be considered. Consumer knowledge is never complete; we only know what we remember (whether we were actually there or only saw it advertised). It takes effort to identify options beyond this. Trade conditions are rarely homogeneous. It takes effort to reconcile different kinds of competitive advantage with different diplomatic relations and different trade mechanisms. The production possibilities curves for any array of products we produce require energy and effort to shift upon. Of course, the field of economics has long known all of this. We humans also know it (deep down in our hearts, I suppose), but my suspicion is that we're not only disinclined to pay attention to the *energy* value of money, we may even be trained to actively overlook that kind of value.

Why consider the entire energetic chain that will hook me onto drug X when I can simply see the ease of people grilling in a sunny park instead? Cute line drawings of placid characters and mesmerizing minimalist music to bypass any inconvenience that may obstruct the consumer's route from "as seen on TV" to "find out more..." There are energetic costs to the investments we make, but those costs can only be properly calculated by the consumer himself. If you don't consider the ongoing underattended costs of your investments, no one else will.

No one else can.

Even if they wanted to.

The Time-*Energy* Value of Money (TEVM) states as follows:

- Money and time are related.

- Energy invested is related to money and time.

- Less money now is preferable to more money later

- *Less money (payoff) at this energy|effort level is preferable to more money at a higher energy level (invested)

- Riskier investments should, if successful, pay more

- More energetically costly investments should, if successful, pay more.

- Time lost is money lost (when energy is constant).

- Time lost is energy saved (when money is held constant).

- Money lost is energy|effort lost (when time invested is held constant).

- Time x Energy invested is proportional to Money gained. $TE = aM$

  - Relatedly, money gained divided by the time it took to earn it is proportional to the rate of energy invested. $E = a\frac{M}{T}$

Although TEVM doesn't exactly state that people are lazy, it does imply that people would prefer less effort to more in pursuing a payoff. But like regular TVM, TEVM does not comprise hard rules. For people who are inherently distraction-averse (effort-focused), more energy invested may come automatically. More importantly, when we introduce a person's psychologically efficacious niche into the picture, more energy and more time come automatically, but not necessarily more money. Why?

BECAUSE MONEY ISN'T THE ONLY FORM OF CAPITAL

As soon as we begin the translation of monetary capital into other forms such as psychological efficacy or emotional fulfillment, we begin to rediscover where a lot of people's payoff actually goes.

Recall that back in the first chapter we claimed that money was a kind of "energy carrier" for publicly agreed upon value. Now we've come full circle with TEVM. Money may be a kind of energy carrier, but not all forms of value can be agreed upon publicly. Of the remaining three kinds of capital, only social capital approaches the level of publicly observable status that money does. Even then, most of the value in social capital lies in its non-observable psychological and emotional components. So although TEVM gets us closer to a proper "rules of thumb" set for assigning value to something, it doesn't go all the way because it still frames money as money instead of just one form of four types of capital. If we replace "money" in the TEVM rules with the word "resources" or the word "capital," we get something more accurate. We also get a more flexible construct for placing the kinds of payoff that may result from a transaction.

A Capital Vector

Vectors in math are essentially an ordered family of numbers. Perhaps you saw this coming, but we would like to represent the value of things using a four-vector instead of a single dollar amount. That is, instead of

representing the price of a thing as $250,000,
We'd like to represent it as something like

<A+ $_{Psychological}$, 250000 $_{Monetary}$, 0.7 $_{Social}$, ∞ $_{Emotional}$>

for that extra fulfilling (∞ $_{Emotional}$) dream
house, which will grant you passable social
status (0.7 $_{Social}$), but make you feel like a boss
(A+ $_{Psychological}$), and costs a mere $250,000
$_{Monetary}$. (The vector is ordered, by the way, from
[0...1 bounded], [0...∞ unbounded], [-1 $_{Them}$...0
$_{You}$...1 $_{Them}$ bounded], [-∞...0...+∞ unbounded].)

The advantage of this kind of
representation is that it makes all of the
returns on your potential purchase clear and
obvious. But you don't need to ask whether
it's fulfillment-fulfillment or satisfaction-
fulfillment you mean, clarifying-social
relationships or familiar ones you mean. You
simply compress all of that into the
appropriate final capital type. And even
though I've included more detail in the above
explanation of 4-dimensional capital, all it is
is a "list" that includes social, emotional, and
psychological value alongside price. Of course,
you wouldn't use all this for everyday
purchases, but for major decisions like moves
and job-changes, a capital vector can help you
to compare your options fully and realistically.

A Slight Adjustment to Our Scales

In order to make balanced decisions which keep our own financial and psychological positions in perspective, it helps to scale the price of things when we value them. The house example above is a little unruly in that it includes two big numbers, a very small one, and a letter. Depending on what your goal is, you may or may not want to scale these for comparison of say, objects that you plan to invest in for later resale. For personal purchases, your subjective liking might be good enough, but for an array of investment objects towards which you are indifferent, scaling may be useful.

An Example:

Suppose you're considering investing in three items: an antique painting, a (badly damaged) classic car, or an ancient sword. They cost $900, $1200, and $700 respectively. You can only buy one, you don't care which, but want the one with the highest return. You determine that the classic car is A LOT more work, but may also be more rewarding and have a much higher return given your ability to fix it. You think the painting is a safe resell, and the sword is freakin' awesome. You don't want to put a lot of work into making a detailed capital vector for each one, but you

DO want to consider the time and effort you'll need to put into making each one into cash. Even a rough capital vector can work like a kind of note-taking on your considerations, so you decide to make some quick lists. (Mark the time. I'm about to start this at 8:21 pm while writing this book.)

Item	Purchase <Psy,Mon,Soc,Em>	Resale <Psy,Mon,Soc,Em>
Painting	< B, 900, 0, 0>	< B, 1600, .3, .1>
Car	< D, 1200, .8, .2>	< A, 10000 after parts, .9, .9 >
Sword	< A, 700, .5, .1 >	< A, 1200, .2, .1>

Finished at 8:25 pm. I've scaled the emotional fulfillment already from 0 (vacuum) to 1 (source).

That was pretty fast, mainly because all I did was assign numbers to how I thought I would feel about the various capital categories. It was only an opinion, and numbers may not capture all of the factors involved (especially the time it takes to fix the car), but at least I've thought enough about the non-monetary aspects of these purchases to assign some kind of value to them. We will factor in the time, by the way, after the next step.

Now even though I've assigned numbers to these purchases, they are still hard to compare because the money values are too large. So I will scale these values by some generic ballpark figure that I'm willing to pay for these items specifically on the current list. Let's call it $1000. Also, changing the psychological grades into numbers 0...1, I obtain the following:

Item	Purchase	Resale
Painting	< .8, .9, 0, 0>	< .8, 1.6, .3, .1>
Car	< .6,1.2,.8,.2>	< .9, 10.0 after parts, .9, .9 >
Sword	< .9, .7, .5, .1 >	< .9, 1.2, .2, .1>

Now let's calculate the return: Resale – Purchase.

Item	Purchase	Resale	Return
Painting	<.8, .9, 0, 0>	< .8, 1.6, .3, .1>	<0, .7, .3, .1 >
Car	<.6,1.2,.8,.2>	< .9, 10.0 after parts, .9, .9 >	<.3, 8.8, .1, .7 >
Sword	< .9, .7, .5, .1 >	< .9, 1.2, .2, .1>	<0, .5, -.3, 0 >

Now is a good time to estimate the effects of the car taking a long time. Suppose it takes 2, 12, and 3 months to sell the painting, car, and sword respectively. Let's divide each item by the time it takes them to pay off.

Item	Purchase	Resale	Return / time invested
Painting	< .8, .9, 0, 0>	< .8, 1.6, .3, .1>	<0, .35, .15, .05 >
Car	< .6, 1.2, .8, .2>	< .9, 10.0 after parts, .9, .9 >	<.03, .73, .08, .06 >
Sword	< .9, .7, .5, .1 >	< .9, 1.2, .2, .1>	<0, .17, -.1, 0 >

On a normal day when working with vectors, we would square each term, take the square root, and obtain magnitudes. But in theory, we have already scaled everything down to a single capital-like measure called "usefulness to us" or utility. We also want to take into account the idea that the sword won't be nearly as cool by the time we sell it, so we don't want to square a negative and turn it positive. The sword must pay the price for losing its luster. Accordingly, all we'll do is add everything up.

Item	Return / time invested	Final usefulness
Painting	<0, .35, .15, .05 >	.55
Car	<.03, .73, .08, .06 >	.90
Sword	<0, .17, -.1, 0 >	.07

So it turns out that the car may be the most valuable IF I can sell it within a year. If, however, I can get a buyer for the painting within one month instead of two, the painting will have a usefulness of 1.1. With just a little more effort that might be a lot quicker. One thing I've learned is that the sword, fancy as it may be, just doesn't stack up as an investment. My consideration of the lost social benefit of having had it along with the stably low fulfillment upon having sold it made a big difference in its *long-term* value.

In the end, I'd probably choose the painting, simply because I don't know cars that well. These numbers are still useful even if you ignore their results though, because they focus your consideration upon what is most important about the investment, including how much or how long your plan to enjoy it. And yes, I made A LOT of assumptions here. (Can we really just *add* different kinds of capital like that?) But the point wasn't to model a government. It was only to build-in other kinds of effort I might need to think about. If I dare to challenge my own initial framing of the capital values and proceed contrary to the 4-D calculations after all, I will at least have given sufficient thought to the whole space of factors involved.

Considering All Capital Forms

Now you may say that was overkill. Maybe it was. Maybe it wasn't. For people who need to quantify large sets of options without necessarily trying out or pouring a lot of thought into each specific one, the capital vector, divided by time, is one way of considering the total effort involved in a potential undertaking.

$$TE = aM \text{ or } E = a\frac{M}{T}$$

becomes

$$E = a \frac{< Psy, Mon, Soc, Em >}{T}$$

and if Psy, Mon, Soc, and Em have been scaled to values between 0...1, simple estimates of (quick and dirty) utility become

$$E = (1) \frac{Psy + Mon + Soc + Em}{T}$$

where E here is something like the rate of energy we can expect to get out of the investment.

References

ways to measure the non-capital aspects 143
Eaton, E. (2011). Let the market decide? Canadian farmers fight the logic of market choice in GM wheat. *ACME: An International E-Journal for Critical Geographies, 10*(1), 107–130.

Whether and how we consider those costs 143
García-Barrios, L., García-Barrios, R., Cruz-Morales, J., & Smith, J. A. (2015). When death approaches: Reverting or exploiting emergent inequity in a complex land-use

table-board game. *Ecology & Society, 20*(2), 154–170.

complex formulas for turning ratings into value 144
Julia, C., & Hercberg, S. (2018). Big food's opposition to the French Nutri-Score front-of-pack labeling warrants a global reaction. *American Journal of Public Health, 108*(3), 318–320.

revolves around the quest to make big purchases 144
Fagundes, D. (2017). Buying happiness: Property, acquisition, and subjective well-being. *William & Mary Law Review, 58*(6), 1851–1931.

Ziegler, C. L., Schmiedl, E., & Callahan, T. (2017). One Mortgage: A model of success for low-income homeownership. *Boston College Environmental Affairs Law Review, 44*(2), 339–360.

time value of money 146
Chiu, Y., & Su, D. (2010). Considering quality cost, time-value of money, and process quality improvement function in the economic product quantity model. *Journal of the Chinese Institute of Industrial Engineers, 27*(4), 249–259.

the amount of energy... to be considered 146
Hamadani, A., & Khorshidi, H. (2013). System reliability optimization using time value of money. *International Journal of Advanced Manufacturing Technology, 66*(1–4), 97–106.

Cute line drawings of placid characters 147
Shah, E. D., Larson, L. R. L., & Denton, L. L. (2019). Animation and consumer perceptions of DTC pharmaceutical advertisement. *Journal of Consumer Affairs, 53*(4), 1456–1477.

less effort to more in pursuing a payoff 149
Traczyk, J., Sobkow, A., Fulawka, K., Kus, J., Petrova, D., & Garcia-Retamero, R. (2018). Numerate decision makers don't use more effortful strategies unless it pays: A process tracing investigation of skilled and adaptive strategy selection in risky decision making. *Judgment & Decision Making, 13*(4), 372–381.

Chapter 10: On the Creation of Micromarkets

Two chapters ago we briefly discussed ways to recruit trading partners to fill in certain deficits in your capital space. The key to recruiting such partners lies in 1) letting them know you're there, 2) telling them what you do and how you prefer to be "paid," and 3) filling in their deficits and accepting their preferred methods of "payment." Now this is all fine and good, but it misses an important third element of any exchange between two actors: the medium over which the exchange takes place. Money is passed through hard currency, banks, or some kind of IOU-recognizing space. Words are passed through air. Internal thoughts are passed across neurons. If we don't have a vehicle for exchange, we tend not to have an exchange. But if we do have a medium of exchange and that same medium is recognized whether you and I trade or Juan and Emma trade, the medium itself becomes a space with a certain capacity for transaction. This leads us to the notion of a market.

It would be so much easier to recruit trading partners if the types of trades we were looking to make were somehow considered legitimate by people other than us. The value in a market is that we are no longer confined to trade our special forms of capital only with each other. If I give you and others emotional satisfaction in exchange for you and them giving me familiar social relationships, a market for that kind of trade allows us to turn around and pass such satisfaction or familiarity onto people beyond ourselves in exchange for still other kinds of capital. Before you know it, these things become a kind of currency for trading in every other good possessable among all of us in the market.

Specifically, having role efficacy (psychological capital) can be especially rewarding. If only you could create a little market in which your specific brand of role efficacy were prized and supported, you might not have to worry about whether anyone would accept your niche talents for a while after that. If you are open- minded enough and farsighted enough, you may be able to create a micromarket for stably trading in your favorite kinds of capital—both including and beyond money. We'll walk through how this is done. But first, you'll need to keep certain rules in mind.

What is A Micromarket?

A market is an exchange space over which resources are traded for other resources in an organized, intentional fashion among the traders. A food fight isn't a market, because being bombed by somebody's banana isn't an organized trade. An angry crowd isn't a market, because even though each shouter may consider himself a resource, his resource isn't consistent enough with other's resources or received consistently enough by others to be considered organized either. In market, a thing of type X is traded for a thing of type Y, both intentionally received, as a regular property of the exchanges there. A micromarket (not to be confused with the vending kind) can be considered the same thing as a traditional market, except for a few components that arise as a consequence of the small number of primary trade partners involved:

- In a micromarket, we assume that it's okay for only one or actor (or relatedly small numbers of actors) to be the unique source of each type of thing.

- We assume that each actor is *obligated* to trade with the other actors in order for the system itself to hold its stable character.

- Finally, trade partners in a micromarket are more likely to be uniquely associated with the things they trade. That is, Person A trades resource A, Person B trades resource B, and Person C trades resource C, all with each other so that the medium of their trades adopts a reasonably stable character in itself.

You can think of a micromarket as a small group of people who combine their skills with each other in order to accomplish something. That something could be money making, or it could just be generic satisfaction in pursuit of some collection of ideals that the members couldn't reach alone. They could feel like friendships, project groups, meetups or businesses, but their whole point is to provide an outlet for each actor's unique A+ niche—a place where everyone else understands how to receive it and gives their own A+ niches in return—typically towards some collective result, formal or otherwise.

The number one reason for forming micromarkets is to *do something* with a talent you definitely have, but one which your job, friends, family, or other resources don't currently, comfortably support. So you paint, but no one around you gives a damn? You're not really trying to be a full blown artist, but you are interested in working with kids and perhaps teaching? You also know someone who teaches side classes on stuff? You might form a micromarket with them. Maybe in money making workshops, or maybe in weekend volunteering at new and interesting places around the city. Micromarkets serve as an outlet for the people in them, mainly towards emotional and psychological fulfillment. You might consider forming one where there is no reasonable alternative outlet for your A+ niche among the other contexts you currently have access to.

Do something with that talent. Talk about it with someone who's in a similar situation with their own talent and exchange yours for theirs. You might even produce some joint result together.

Why Form Micromarkets?

The benefit of a micromarket is that the actors in it find reasonably reliable demanders or vacuums for the types of fulfillment objects which they possess in oversupply, thus facilitating continued or increased role efficacy, relationship building, general fulfillment, or monetary exchange. Without such micromarkets, these same actors often have no choice but to trade with the hit and miss demand of the external public which may or may not reliably reward their niches—only their jobs or other socially recommended obligations.

If you and a few companions can successfully design a micromarket for your respective niches, you will essentially gain a stable space of "buyers" (receivers, or time-energy exchangers) for things you actually do well. That is, the interpersonal version of your "competitive advantage" will actually have some place to go if you haven't found this already. You will also gain a stable space of suppliers for your specific capital deficits—areas where you are a natural demander or vacuum for fulfillment with respect to a certain kind of resource.

What You'll Need In Order To Build a Micromarket

To build a micromarket from nothing, you will almost certainly need two major pieces:

1. A partner who is not just willing to trade with you, but who is interested enough in the idea of trading with you even though you may have no existing overarching

framework for generating any kind of collective value. You start with nothing. They start with nothing. And you're both okay with this.

a. It really helps if they are interested in the *idea*. Not necessarily in partnering with you as a person, friend, or social associate. Unless they are already easy trading partners in yours and their oversupplies and deficits, their interest in things besides the idea may complicate your aim to find "buyers and suppliers" for the capital you seek. Trust me, I've learned this one the hard way. As is the case when starting businesses with friends, starting a micromarket with people who don't understand what you're actually trying to exchange...has a decent chance of complicating things later on. You *will* need to like each other, and I'll talk about this shortly. But you'll also need to map a clear path for yourselves on the road ahead.

b. Now, if you're starting your trade group with someone who already makes a good capital partner in both yours and their deficits and oversupplies, you might ask *What good is a market?*

(You'll already have a kind of closed "economy" between the two of you.) And that's a good question. For the purposes of expansion, you'll often need room to add other kinds of traders. Especially a monetary trader later on.

2. The second thing you'll need is a vision for what your market produces overall. This is your trader's collective "export." It is also the thing for which the external world will pay your market members. Your market's accepted form of payment is the fuel that enables your market members to keep working with each other even as family issues, bills, illness, and other personal demands exert their pull on your little group. As your market group evolves, if it endures long enough, you'll likely experience every event that regular employees at a regular job will experience, and your market will need to survive those things the way a regular job would. But the reason you've even bothered to build this market was because you wanted to supplement the money you got from your regular job with a genuine place of fulfillment for your unique role efficacy. It's easy to forget this if all you've come to do is play with each other, and just as easy to

forget if you expect to just magically morph into a traditional business with traditional services. Your group needs an export that fits the talents of the people in it. That export won't always be a sellable thing, and anyone who wants to be a member of your market has to be on board with whatever you've chosen to create together. It won't be a regular job, but will take the same level of mutual cooperation that a regular job would.

Hard Facts About Making Micromarkets

As intentionally designed niche-swapping groups of *individuals*, micromarkets are, by definition, fragile. At least in the beginning. Our Western economy is full of better (-looking) choices. Our spaces of friends are full of people who, ironically, know less about who we really want to be and more about who they're used to *thinking* we are—the only sides we consistently reaffirm to them. So when you tell friends and family, "I want to be an actress" or "I plan to build a random little group for myself," the kind of support you get is likely to be more of the obligated verbal kind than the active "Let me help you do it" kind. Friends and family often won't get it, because your new idea may not resemble closely enough the common frameworks that have contributed to your default socially accepted roles up to that point. That's not intended to be cynicism. It's just the nature of many people's responses when you suddenly decide to create something they've never seen or heard about before—especially from you.

Typically then, your micromarket (at least in the early 21st century West) may only find active support among the people willing to jump right into the market with you. Your other friends and family won't actively discourage you, but many may do their best to protect you from disappointment, from your market partners, from risk, from things, people, and process that they (and by assumption, you) don't know. Not all micromarket makers will experience this, but if you're reading this and you're thinking about creating your own uniquely-matched trade space, don't be surprised if you encounter all of this and then some.

Now, you might think that micromarkets required a lot of "expertise" to assemble. They don't. Even if you choose to adopt a formal business structure like an LLC or Corporation for your group, there is plenty of good guidance out there to help you through. You'll find out that places like the IRS are actually pretty supportive in the training and other help they provide. Additionally, you will be building your market with partners who are already niche specialists willing and able to trade their role efficacy basically infinitely. So no, expertise isn't necessarily something you'll need to worry about. You may, however, as one of the founding members of the market, be responsible for the recordkeeping, basic legalities, and running agreements in your group. This can sometimes feel like more of an oppressive business setup than a rewarding niche space for you the founder, so you may want to bring in someone who loves those kinds of tasks—whose passion is organization. Given that you have the capacity to organize the efforts of others towards the overall group vision, you're now ready for the real rules of micromarkets.

1. **Micromarkets**, in their single-supplier specificity, **can't feel like jobs.** They really do have to feel like fun most of the time. Ultimately, the ideal micromarket consists of people at the A+ top of their role efficacy, with their own unique niches in oversupply. No one else in the market has the knowledge to tell them how to use that niche, and no one else in the market can motivate the niche-holder's obsessive

hobby more than the holder themselves can.

2. **Don't expect to be paid in money.** Especially if money wasn't the deficit or oversupply you formed the market to trade in in the first place. This only becomes obvious after you've found out that you needed money to buy things, or wanted money in exchange for your groups' exports. But if your market doesn't begin with its roots in money making, don't expect this to change until you bring a niche money-trader into your group. Until that time comes, don't worry too much about it. Don't spend dough stupidly, but paychecks are what day jobs are for. There's no need to force your non-job niche to care about it if it's just not natural to do so. Your market should be mostly fun, remember?

And now for the serious rules:

3. **You'll need to get along.** A micromarket trades skills like a business, but no one in it can be forced to trade. Unless you've gotten so formal that you've evolved a system of contracts, any essential member can walk out for any reason whatsoever. Just because they're tired of you. Try to get

along. Failure to do so can make things extra nasty when more than one super niche-effective, founding visionary is involved.

4. **You'll need to trust each other's judgment.** Everyone knows "that idea" the other day was yours. But if you knew everything, you wouldn't need a market of mutual experts now, would you? If you brought that expert on to do a specific thing, you probably want to let them do their thing. This is as true for the highest role as it is for the lowest role in your market. Don't treat the notetaker like garbage. Respect his or her way of handling things. Unless you want to file those tax documents on your own.

5. **You'll need to respect each other's choices.** This is similar to the above rule, but applied after the fact. If one of your market members has done something that you don't agree with, messed something up, or dropped the ball, you need to try try try to forgive them. People in real markets and real jobs mess up all the time. But you've got a team full of people who are known for trying their best in their roles. As easy as it is for a founder to take that for granted, ask yourself whether you'd

rather have those mediocre performers outside of your market circumscribing your dream niche instead. No one's going to die. It's not that serious. Errors *can't be* that serious if you want your market to survive.

6. **If ever there are difficulties among you, you'll need to talk them out.** In a micromarket,

   a. silence is a trade sanction.

   b. Going AWOL installs a blackhole which others *must* fulfill instantly.

   c. One-sided conversations make for one-sided skill-trading.

None of this will help any of you. In the construction of my first micromarket, I lost one major founding member to each of these events. If we can't talk, we can't trade. At that point, everyone's niches, whatever they may be, become invisible to the market as a whole. Even if you try to keep up communication with a subgroup among the members, if you can't trade with every other member, your days in the market are basically numbered. Accordingly,

7. **everyone in a micromarket should ideally be open to trading with everyone else.** And even though the market founders don't necessarily hold superior positions over the other market members, people who aren't willing to trade with the founders themselves should NEVER be allowed into the market while it's still in infancy. If you try letting someone with an attitude into your group, be prepared for a world of trouble trying to pry them back out of your group. The market is based on a mutual vision. People who join the market with their own individual interests, rather than the additional interests of the group in mind, tend to wreak of "let's do it my way"-style mutiny before they begin. Leave the blinders at home. Just because someone has a skill, doesn't mean you should allow them to jerk up your scene through their combat with certain members or ego-boosting off of others.

8. **Settle conflicts with the overall vision in mind.** Did another member upset you? Okay. But what happens when your micromarket breaks down? Who will complement your dream role then? Who's going to put up with your crazy ideas then? Your job? Your protectively alliance-

dividing friends? Your family who insists they told you so? Get it together and do what you can to keep this super unique thing alive. Which leads us to the final rule...

9. **In the event of a partnership-fatal conflict, the last person who typically tried in earnest, through compromise, to hold the union together is typically the one who retains access to the dream.** The one who walked out, typically proves they will walk out on the next opportunity like it. The dream is far less likely to arrive for them, even if they do start something of their own. If a person can't compromise they just can't compromise. Yet compromise amidst a sea of unique potentials is the foundation of a free market. If you and your fellow members can talk out your difficulties with the overall vision in mind, you may eventually come to resemble more of a family than trading partners. My first micromarket suffered three fatal exits, mainly because of problems with rules 6 & 8. But that market is still standing, having lived long enough to publish this book. Your market partners are rarely angels, yet they tend to be as visionary as you allow

yourself to be. The group you launch truly has the potential to stand apart from any other thing you've ever known. If you and your partners can see it through, you will have created something that no one else has or can. It's worth it to keep fighting for your dream's survival.

The Market Has Its Own Direction

We're done with the serious rules, and now (on a lighter note) we'll discuss a couple of cool things you might not expect from your market.

Although you may be tempted to run your market like a business, you shouldn't marry yourself too much to the idea.

- The basic function of a business is to provide a service in exchange for money. Thus, monetary capital tends to be a built-in priority for businesses.

- Furthermore, the specific talents of the business' employees are deemphasized in favor of the kinds of skills that the business itself requires. You may be a brilliant painter, but can you use this here customer software?

- Businesses have an implied duty hierarchy, where the product or service is the focus. In micromarkets, the product-*maker* is the focus. If there is any duty hierarchy, it is aimed at the sustainment of relationships among the group members, not sustainment of the members' wares.

- In businesses, the people are replaceable, the product line less so. In a micromarket, the people can be replaced with a little more difficulty, but the early product line is VERY replaceable as the people figure out how to plug their niches into each other's. As for the niche exports themselves, these will change with the people. The founders may need to do a little bit of juggling to keep the group's export as stable-looking to the public as possible, even as changes in members radically alter the skill sets (and outputs) available to them.

In the end, it's the vision for certain kinds of dynamics that characterize a micromarket, but an average consumer isn't trained to understand vision nearly as easily as he understands product offerings. As a result, your market may morph repeatedly, eluding early explanation among your public. Don't let it get to you though. Just keep working with your fellow market members to produce something that highlights everyone's A+ role, and does justice to the collective. People will likely see it and give you some embodiment of their attention accordingly.

In line with the kinds of trades we were built upon, my partners' and my market was paid very little in monetary capital, but paid A LOT in social capital in exchange for our oversupply in communicated impressions. And this leads me to the most fun aspect of all when it comes to micromarkets.

- Unlike a business, your market will evolve like any other thing you create under your psychological niche. It will absorb every significant partner of yours—temporary or long term—as one of its creative parents, and will eventually reflect the tapestry of their contributions. In this way, micromarkets resemble works of art beneath a business-looking shell. The longer you nurture them with good relations, big dreams, and patience, the prouder of your market you're more likely to be.

Where Do You Start?

1. For building a group of collaborators with no real money in sight, I highly recommend

the book *Slicing Pie* by Mike Moyer. It talks all about how you can take a venture with no real value and assign it virtual value in a fair way, with different kinds of treatment for different levels of risk assumed by all the parties involved. Time, credit lines, ownership equity, hourly rates, stakes in lieu of payment...it's in there. But the most important message in the book revolves around fairness. Get familiar with fairness and transparency before you begin the ride with others. It will go a very long way.

2. Find a partner who is willing to trade with you, who is interested in the *idea*, who demands some (but not all) of what you have in oversupply and gives some (but not all) of what you demand in deficit.

3. With the person above and your basic trade objects determined, agree upon a vision—a collective "export"—along with a basic culture for such export that guides you market's evolution. What do we mean by culture? That is simply the attitude you take towards each other and your shared work. Is it fun? Intense? Sociable? My own micromarket has bits of these, but mainly revolves around a culture of "Through your perfected creativity anything is possible, no

matter what obstacles you begin with. It's our role to make that known to everyone everywhere." Your culture can be captured in a single word, an entire mission statement, or through actions that go beyond words.

4. Work together to produce something that is bigger than either of your efforts alone. Don't worry about money unless it was one of your designated trade objects or you *need* it to purchase certain resources.

5. Show others what you've created. Don't just sit on it.

6. Locate newer trade partners that complement your current group and fill in critical vacancies in your skill set. Ensure that each new person you add gets along with <u>everyone else</u> already in the group and that they accept and fully support the vision of the market. Not just themselves.

7. If you intend to replace your day jobs with this activity, keep creating whatever you create until you can afford to add a money-trader to your group (an [oversupply Other-to-them attractor] or a [deficit Them-to-other puller]).

Is that all? Yes. This doesn't have to be complicated. Only the introduction of money and legalities, when your market gets to that point, will put you through a potentially challenging phase if these weren't part of your initial market—but are now inherited by necessity. Keep the vision in mind and set your sights on the appropriate traders to add to your market. Talk out any conflicts and keep the dream going. Remember, if you let it break, all you may have left is the tried and true "boxed life" you originally hoped to leave behind.

References

confined to trade...only with each other 162
Malloy, T. F. (2002). Regulating by incentives: Myths, models, and micromarkets. *Texas Law Review, 80*(3), 531.

create a little market in which... 162
Seman, M., & Carroll, M. C. (2017). The creative economies of Texas metropolitan regions: A comparative analysis before, during, and after the recession. *Growth & Change, 48*(4), 831–852.

generic satisfaction in pursuit of... 164
Lyons, M., & Snoxell, S. (2005). Sustainable urban livelihoods and marketplace social

capital: Crisis and strategy in petty trade. *Urban Studies, 42*(8), 1301–1320.

thus facilitating... 165

Romer, P. (1990). Endogenous technological change. *Journal of Political Economy 98*(5), S71–S102.

space of suppliers for your specific... deficits 166

Ren, Y., Xia, T., Li, Y., & Chen, X. (2019). Predicting socio-economic levels of urban regions via offline and online indicators. *PLoS ONE, 14*(7), 1–15.

an export that fits the talents of... 169

Güzel, D., Kabakuş, A. K., & Sirin, M. S. (2018). A value stream mapping implementation: A case of textile industry. *Ataturk University Journal of Economics & Administrative Sciences, 32*(3), 763–772.

...like the IRS are actually pretty supportive 170

IRS. n.d. IRS videos. Retrieved January 8, 2020 from https://www.irsvideos.gov/

don't expect this to change... 172

Boamah, M. I. (2019). Inflation dynamics in a small developing economy: An empirical analysis for Ghana. *Journal of Developing Areas, 53*(3), 229–237.

Slicing Pie 180

Moyer, M. (2012). Slicing pie: Funding your company without funds. Lake Shark.

Chapter 11: A Comment on American Social Tiers

I was blessed to grow up with people of nearly every combination of race, education level, and socioeconomic tier. I've lived, taught, and worked with people ranging from the very rich and very educated to the very poor and minimally trained. Over the years I've made some observations about these classes which you might find interesting. They're not rooted in statistics, but you may find their overall patterns familiar.

In working with college data I've found it convenient to divide our social populations into six basic socioeconomic status (SES) tiers:

- Poor
- Lower Middle Class
- Middle Class
- Lower Upper Class
- Rich
- Ultra Rich

My observations of these classes is one you probably already suspected. They may or may not agree with your experiences:

Middle Class

The Middle Class constitutes the workhorse of a general economy. Its members earn median household incomes, consume the goods which are overwhelmingly targeted to them, spend the expected discretionary income, and make the big inefficient purchases aimed at bringing them closer to Upper Class-style living. They don't generally invest efficiently, carry the typical debts, and are generally ineffective at actively influencing social and political policy, mainly because they don't know they can. They vote as prescribed, in the usual numbers for the usual options, and can be expected to not ask questions about what their social and civic options are or why they are. This is the tier I've spent most of my life on.

Middle Class life is overwhelmingly one of endless striving to be richer, to finally get out of work through retirement, and spend as much fun time with friends as our grinding lives has made us feel entitled to. We do have goals though, and tend to anchor into friends and family in circling around those goals, even if we never reach them. If we could simply be more like the Upper Class, we're certain our lives would be easier. We hope never to be afflicted with a health event or layoff that would plunge us into the Lower Middle Class. But if that does happen, we often opt to share our living spaces with other Middle Classers or split the cost of the lifestyle with Lower Upper and Rich landlords who charge us at least 20% more than we should be paying (as that is a passable rate of return for them), even as we only command Lower Middle Class monetary worth. At least we still *look* the part.

Lower Upper Class

The Upper Class consists of several levels: Lower Upper Class, the Rich, and Ultra Rich. If a Middle Class person does manage to save, typically marries, has a manager, medical, longer-term military, tech person, or other socially advantageous job among the earners, or is simply good-looking or otherwise socially favorable, their chances of moving from the Middle Class to the Lower Upper class are much higher. This tier has almost invariably saved more, is better educated, lives in what Middle Classers refer to as "nice neighborhoods," and can do things like dine out and take vacations in the low $1000s of dollars. Lower Upper Classers aren't quite rich, though. Their debt-to income is comparable to that of Middle Classers, except with bigger numbers, though their retirement and interest in investments tend to be a lot higher.

Much more than Middle Classers, however, Lower Upper Classers actively care about the livability of their communities. So they are more concerned with crime, education, and neighborhood transformation, are more likely to volunteer. They are also more likely to assemble with others on the basis of shared status (as opposed to common perspective). Often, this is not necessarily a good thing.

I've observed that a Lower Upper Class couple is more likely to have close friends who don't so much see eye to eye with them on deep issues the way Middle Classers, the Poor, and the Rich do. Instead they are more likely to inherit friends through their SES tier. Among many Lower Upper Classers, there are the shared social activities common to the class, but fewer true friends in other households. The lower tiers tend to have more truly supportive friends, for reasons I'll speculate about shortly. A lot of this has to do with what makes a household "Lower Upper Class" to begin with: More money and security than the Middle, but less social license than the Rich.

From what I've seen, the Lower Upper Class is one of the two most money-defensive classes (along with the Rich), ever with its back towards the Middle Class and its more immediate societal concerns. The Lower Upper Class, in my observation is also, broadly, one of the two classes whose members have the lowest general happiness with their lives. Often, much of their SES-mobile civic attention is spent measuring their accomplishments by looking down on the two classes immediately beneath them while looking up through the lens of what their higher capital worth allows them to buy. These aren't statistics, I remind you, just a pattern I've observed in my travels. It can be difficult to talk to a Lower Upper Classer about the advantages they have—namely prosocial characteristics like good looks, good families, and parents or associates who connected them—as they will swear they've earned what they've earned through their own hard work. It will be harder to convince them that the Lower Middle Class man in construction or the poverty-level woman who is a server also work hard too, as the deaf ears often settle in quickly when you begin discussing personal disadvantages that often could not have been controlled for. The difference between Lower Upper Classers and other people on the tiers beneath them often rests on these personal social advantages: Those above Middle Class frequently had them. Those capped at Middle Class frequently didn't. But you can't tell a Lower Upper Classer that.   That would defy the American Dream they've managed to make real, wouldn't it?

Lower Middle Class

The Lower Middle Class *would* be Middle Class, except their credit is terrible; they have been compelled to live with extra family members, housemates, or roommates; are more likely to be out of work for critical stretches of time or work on a half-time, low benefits basis; they have low balances in their checking accounts; and think a lot about bills. They don't quite always live paycheck to paycheck, for many have paychecks that are just too low to live on. Others do make enough, but live in ways which help their money evaporate into any number of common consumer outlets. As a result, they are more likely to be supported by Middle Class connections or other Lower Middle Class connections. Accordingly, members of this tier may live in decent places like apartments or houses, and even hold decent-looking jobs.

But they struggle to get beyond where they are financially.

So what stops the Lower Middle from saving, spending more wisely or otherwise moving up? The answer might surprise you. As far as I've observed, Lower Middle Classers form the socioeconomic tier whose members are the happiest with themselves and who they are. The incentive to truly pursue more monetary capital comes in third behind the social and emotional capital that they already have where they are. This tier might be described as comfortable, but don't confuse that with laziness.

The Lower Upper Rich and above may not believe that the Lower Middle Class could possibly be happy and near-broke simultaneously, until they spend time with a Lower Middle Class social circle for an extended period of time. Select domestic issues may arise, and the interactional roller coaster tends to be more apparent among the Lower Middle Class, but so is the caring. There is less of a sense that "we are stuck together because of this lifestyle" and more of a sense that "we aren't necessarily stuck together, but I want to be here even when you aggravate me." Formal separations are higher, but social separations are lower. The social and emotional capital are richer even if the monetary capital isn't, ironically because the Lower Middle Classer's socioeconomic dependence on others forces him or her to respect the value in a strong social tie.

I've often said that if I could take the spirit of a Lower Middle Classer with me, I might be more comfortable pursuing the American notion of "rich." We pursue the American Rich because our consumer market punishes us if we don't. But when it comes to individuals looking in the mirror and loving the people they've become, American Lower Middle Classers seem to be happier than most groups broadly, while Lower Upper Classers and the American Rich seem to be the two unhappiest tiers of all. Don't believe me? Look at the kinds of personalities that appear in the media typical of each tier. Reality isn't quite the same, but it's not so different either. Look for genuine happiness with oneself, beyond the occasional superior, well-furnished attitude by some, and look for the kind of happiness that is not sponsored by the economic goods or symbols of privilege surrounding the person.

Remove all of the nice furniture, greenery, and obligated self-assuredness and you'll see it too. Some people are fine as they are even if they never get that dreamhouse which was supposed to solve it all.

Poor

The Poor are self-explanatory. They don't make enough, are much more likely to live with others or be taken care of by others, are often out of work but also not under nearly as much pressure *to* work as one might think. Because it pays more to collect assistance, Medicaid, Unemployment, or some other external funding source than it does to scour for menial jobs.

Many of us on the Middle Class tiers or above are inclined to look at the poor and cite them as lazy. Indeed, I've met, taught and, lived around poorer groups, and many poor are lazy. As are many other tier types. More than anything, though, our social security, medical benefits, and assistance structures—in the same way that they are meant to help those in need—also encourage people who wouldn't otherwise need it to highlight the aspects of their lives where they do. So maybe I don't really need unemployment, but I do, ya know? That's what it's there for. This tier is fairly neutral in how it sees the world, though it has almost no socio-political voice save for the issues raised by the tiers above it. Poor tier members are less likely to be blinded by the nature of the capitalist system, can't afford to spend like Middle Classers, but don't perceive the fantasy of equality the way the Lower Upper and the Rich tend to. Overwhelmingly, they *know* the socioeconomic world isn't fair and equal. They know of the jobs they may never get a chance to apply for because of one discriminatory trait or another. They are more *visibly* confronted with society's various problems of domestic and substance abuse, family trauma, food and housing scarcity. They are also more likely to have the existence of their entire tier exploited by various industries who thrive off of certain goods, social services, billing systems, employment practices, and legal pathways. The Poor may not earn much as individuals, but make for a lucrative investment among certain Rich. Thus their persistence at the poverty level is continually supported by higher tiers, regardless of how "lazy" the higher tiers claim the poor themselves to be.

Ultra Rich

The Ultra Rich, in my observation, no longer have anything to prove where the American Dream is concerned. They tend to have and reasonably command enough money to be beyond a drop in SES, so there is a much lower need to define themselves by looking down. Instead, the Ultra Rich are more likely to concentrate their efforts on their own personal visions, be these political, humanitarian, entrepreneurial, or leisure-social related. It's easy for us Americans to admire the Ultra Rich, but harder for us to emulate them, because in order to live as though money is no object, you have to *think* as though money is no object—for your self-definition, that is. Lower Middle, Middle, Lower Upper, and Rich striving for the "Dream"—the *striving* part—very often precludes this. And even though not all members of the Ultra Rich are sages, this tier is more likely to hold people who have a tower view of the world beyond their own bank accounts. The key, I think, lies in this tier's completion of the monetary capital struggle, and more encouraged movement into the quest for psychological capital. *With my billions, am I able to make a difference?* With greater psychological and social capital comes a weakening of money's all-pervading influence—also part of the reason why Lower Middle Classers have seemed to be happy with themselves broadly. If within your circle of influence, big or small, you can think of yourself as role-effective, you are less likely to measure such internalized niche-effectiveness against an external tool. For the Lower Middle and the Ultra Rich classes, no amount of reasonably earnable money will re-align you with the classic American Dream anytime soon. The Middle, Lower Upper, and Rich are too close to that dream, such that the risk of losing access to it is more immediate, making these tiers unhappier broadly, and exploitable broadly. By various industries, assorted social pressures, and by each other.

In a separate vein are the Poor. For them, the American Dream may be exactly that.

Rich

The Rich, in the most vexing economic byproduct of all, reflect so much of what we want, have so much of what we'd like, but are also tasked with administering the systems over which they have control. Having often promoted the socially favorable Lower Upper Class members into their trusted positions, the Rich are *the* tier responsible for most of the operations of corporations, civic administrative structures, regional and multi-location entities, and other wide managerial realms. But there is a price to such influence.

As a group, the Rich have more social and political power than any other group, including the much smaller, much less present-world-practical Ultra Rich group. So they are faced with building systems that cooperate across opposition lines, and for the good of the whole. Consider, however, that a District Manager of Company X isn't paid to decide for the good of the whole. She's paid to decide in favor of Company X. That's her lobby. She isn't motivated to innovate on behalf of the Middle Class. One, she likely never wants to fall to Middle Class status and two, her fellow rich have more important interests to attend to. The problem with the American Rich class is that our celebrated principles of self-determination, spread across a sea of people whose self-interest competes which each other's, leaves us with immeasurable collective power, but very little individual empower*ment*. So although I am powerful within my company, stable enough economically to turn towards sociopolitical activity the way the Ultra Rich do, I'm not influential enough to out-argue the hundreds of thousands of other Rich out there whose opinions differ from mine. Furthermore, I build alliances that reinforce my own social position, so it doesn't occur to me that my Lower Middle and Middle Class stakeholders and neighbors might actually add strength to my voice, if only I represented what they needed rather than expansions upon what I

already have. And then there is the issue of
framing. Because I do have a prosocial
position (the status that comes with money), I
find it harder to relate to the many people I
would never talk to, never hire, in whose
neighborhoods I would never drive, whom I
would never want to be. I want the
psychological efficacy that comes with making
a difference, but the Dream has convinced me
that the "difference" is somehow connected to
my own, uniquely SES-elevated viewpoint. So I
speak for the same two parties, the same
menu of choices, the same providers of my
paycheck, and the same array of issues put
before me by the same general universe of
people who have had the voice and not known
it for over 200 years: people like me. I may
have tried to change the system, but haven't
yet realized that I'm attempting to change
people like myself—and that change of this
type, on this level, is probably not systemic in
nature. It's social. It's not the policy or the
other party that needs changing. It's my
ability to cooperate with them as they are, and
shape us both towards something better. I am
a part of the upper 20%, so there are at least
60 million other Americans who have what I
have. Whether I and others on this tier can
use our positions to improve life for the other

80% is more within my own power of choice than I may realize.

The American Rich are our society's most powerful group. Relatedly, they are also the ones most heavily responsible for the change that does or doesn't happen in society. Under the encouragement to keep striving for individual, short-term interests instead of wider, long-term ones, and faced with a wall of people like themselves in confined perspectives like their own, the best this class has typically been able to do is perpetuate and follow—especially politically. The results of this class' overall discontentment manifest through media, endlessly money-reaching capital practice, and see-sawing policy, where those without such power can only watch the socially strong diminish themselves.

This certainly doesn't describe all Rich. It may not even describe most. It does, however, describe my observations of the Rich Class *as a whole.* Even if this class actually did consist of 80% altruistic freedom fighters, the *collective* result, at the time of this writing, is still a team full of star players running a clearly losing record.

At the time of this writing, it is the ironically "exploited" Middle Class and a subset of the Lower Upper Class which is sponsoring more positive social change as whole groups. Not because its individual members have so much political power. (As I've said, they don't.) But because collectively, they have been compelled to respond vocally to the many technological and social issues that have changed our society but have been brought about from sources beyond their apparent control. Their individual happiness may be another matter, but where training in the collective voice is concerned, the prime consumers of the Dream have, in recent years, demanded that the Dream be rewritten to be more attentive to consumer empowerment. It's a promising lesson in broad cultural teaching that seems to be gaining momentum in these classes as a whole, though there are of course individuals on all economic tiers who are doing their part.

Changing Our Views

Across all SES tiers, there is a common trait that the happiest people possess. You've heard it before: It's their attitude. Attitude is non-capital in nature, but if it were commodifiable, it would be either emotional or psychological in nature depending on whether you were looking inward at your experiences or outward at your effectiveness. Regardless of tier, people who are empowered anywhere they are put—those with high psychological capital—are less likely to perceive obstacles to their individual interests. Part of building psychological capital entails creating an environment in which your unique framework is always a currency accepted.

In the previous chapter I talked about the creation of micromarkets, and how such markets serve as a space in which the things you have in oversupply and the things you constantly need supplied to you both constitute staples of your exchange system with a select group of others. When it comes to building a better society, I've found nothing more rewarding than building a micromarket of my own, and encourage you to consider doing the same. A micromarket takes your area of specialty and pairs it with others' specialty areas, towards the assembly of a type of project which is much greater than any of you could have built alone. While on that project, you also complement each other's weaknesses—where a person not so good at advertising gets advertising help from a person not so good at networking, and so on... Your micromarket can produce a product, a social change group, a work of art, a show, a circle of service provision, or any other kind of alliance that fits your group's particular skills, and will do wonders for your sense of personal empowerment in the process. Revisit Chapter 10 to see how it's done.

I believe that small groups of empowered, mutually supportive people may hold the key to long-lasting social benefit. Since the establishment of my colleagues' and my micromarket, it has been MUCH harder to be bothered by the various, occasionally chaotic happenings in the world beyond us. Maybe you can see why. If you know that you're doing everything you can to be a better, more effective person to yourself and others, if you're building something that puts your maximum usefulness out there for the rest of the world's benefit, no political or social rancor can divert your attention from things you can actually, constantly, positively affect.

Our politics and economy will always be there. It's a good system, I think. We take it for granted because we're not trained in how to effectively share that system with people unlike us and still get valuable work done. Creating a micromarket will shake you out of much of your entrenchment even as it evolves you as a person and a partner. It starts with an appreciation for value which extends beyond the monetary, and your assessment of your own individual power against those more flexible standards.

(This chapter was purposely written full of opinions, but if you are interested in seeing what the more formal research has to say about these issues presented here, see the References below.)

References

is less of a sense that "we are stuck together... 203

Thiele, M., & Gillespie, B. J. (2017). Social stratification at the top rung. *Sociological Perspectives, 60*(1), 113–131.

It's their attitude. 200

Zagonari, F. (2016). Which attitudes will make us individually and socially happier and healthier? A cross-culture and cross-development analytical model. *Journal of Happiness Studies, 17*(6), 2527–2554.

are less likely to perceive obstacles 201

Grafton, B., & MacLeod, C. (2017). A positive perspective on attentional bias: Positive affectivity and attentional bias to positive information. *Journal of Happiness Studies, 18*(4), 1029–1043.

may hold the key to long-lasting... 202

Bucher, A., Neubauer, A. B., Voss, A., & Oetzbach, C. (2019). Together is better: Higher committed relationships increase life satisfaction and reduce loneliness. *Journal of Happiness Studies, 20*(8), 2445–2469.

what the more formal research has to say

Aknin, L. B., Sandstrom, G. M., Dunn, E. W., & Norton, M. I. (2011). It's the recipient that counts: Spending money on strong social ties leads to greater happiness than spending on weak social ties. *Plos One, 6*(2), e17018.

Avin, C., Lotker, Z., Peleg, D., Pignolet, Y.-A., & Turkel, I. (2018). Elites in social networks: An axiomatic approach to power balance and Price's square root law. *PLoS ONE, 13*(10), 1–35.

Džuka, J. (2019). Low-income people and their SWB: Multiple mediational role of two basic psychological needs. *Ceskoslovenska Psychologie, 63*(4), 402–412.

Gleibs, I. H., Morton, T. A., Rabinovich, A., Haslam, S. A., & Helliwell, J. F. (2013). Unpacking the hedonic paradox: A dynamic analysis of the relationships between financial capital, social capital and life satisfaction. *British Journal of Social Psychology, 52*(1), 25–43.

Jasielska, D., Prusik, M., & Rajchert, J. (2019). "I will help but not everybody" - Donating to charity in a deficit vs. growth condition: The Importance of well-being. *Studia Psychologica, 61*(4), 230–244.

Nicolao, L., Irwin, J. R., & Goodman, J. K. (2009). Happiness for sale: Do experiential purchases make consumers happier than material purchases? *Journal of Consumer Research, 36*(2), 188–198.

Oldfield, K. (2007). Expanding economic democracy in American higher education: A two-step approach to hiring more teachers from poverty- and working-class backgrounds. *Journal of Higher Education Policy & Management, 29*(2), 217–230.

Rauscher, E., & Elliott, W. (2016). The relationship between income and net worth in the United States: A virtuous cycle for high- but not low-income households. *Journal of Poverty, 20*(4), 380–395.

Roszkowski, M. J., & Grable, J. (2007). How are income and net worth related to happiness? *Journal of Financial Service Professionals, 61*(1), 64–80.

Ruan, J. (2017). Interaction rituals in guanxi practice and the role of instrumental li. *Asian Studies Review, 41*(4), 664–678.

Spencer, B., & Castano, E. (2007). Social class is dead. Long live social class! stereotype threat among low socioeconomic status individuals. *Social Justice Research, 20*(4), 418–432.

Wiesel, I., & Levin, I. (2018). Cohesion and differentiation in Australia's elite suburbs. *Geographical Research, 56*(4).

Chapter 12: Micro-Collective Funding: A Proposed Solution for Social Inequity

In recent years, my native city of San Antonio, TX has earned the distinction of overtaking Detroit, MI as the most economically segregated city in the US. If you live here, you know why this is. To make a long story short, San Antonio is a big city with a small town feel. It's relatively cheap to live in, is great for retirement with its military and family-centric culture, and features seemingly limitless, prime opportunities for people coming from more expensive places like California to carve up new industry and development space while making a killing further gentrifying the many less affluent neighborhoods the farther away from Northwest and Northeast you go. When it comes to buying low and selling high, San Antonio is what you might call a no-brainer, and will be for years to come.

The next few paragraphs provide a gross generalization of San Antonio. They are unscientific as far as scholarly statements are concerned, and represent the opinions of only one person. They are, however, intended to give you a broad look at some of the heavy *social* factors that have made SA the country's most economically segregated city, as told from the perspective of someone who has had typically had to work harder to be mobile here.

Having spent most of my life in San Antonio, I can honestly say that I prefer it to most other places I've been. The family and clique-centered culture, heavily influenced by its American-Mexican foundations is double-edged, in some places playing out as genuine warmth towards perceived insiders and in other places playing out as basic prejudice towards outsiders. As you might guess, race and class issues come with this.

- The "black box" for the social mobility of my own group is very real if you're not rich, where blacks are distrusted more and more likely to be treated as such—for reasons that must have existed before I was born.

- Non-Spanish speaking Latinx often face a certain level of shaming for this depending on where you go. As do Mexicans and Mexican Americans under the current sociopolitical climate.

There are lots of in-your-face questions like "You are, uh, a citizen, aren't you?" happening these days. Is this wrong, right, or just an innocent inquiry? I wouldn't know. But I do know we weren't asking it nearly as much five years ago. Nor were the ethnically divisive elements in the country as a whole nearly as overt. It's one of those things that some people claim is an innocent question. But you imagine going into a place socio-politically dominated by some skin color other than yours—with talk of voter fraud, jobs, and walls clearly tilted against your kind; from regular people, you additionally get "the question." At the very least, it's tacky.

• On the other end, whites, like everyone else, come in very rich or very poor flavors, and everything in between. But where whites divide economically, the economic dividing lines spanning the city as a whole become more obvious. That is, the wealth of the whites in a San Antonio area tell you more about the wealth of that region on the whole.

But putting the above note on Latinx aside, there is a heavy undercurrent of white-shaming here in San Antonio as well. As though being white automatically obligates a person to be on their best behavior regarding anything race-related. And never say you're proud to be white. Blacks like myself say we're proud to be black all the time. (I do.) The whole city is pretty broadly, proudly, Hispanic in culture and favor. We talk of equality, but whites are discouraged from talking equally on such matters—lest they be thrown into the racist bin. San Antonio has that problem too: It's the call for equity without equality I suppose. Someone should wish us luck on that.

- Experiences averaged across the city as a whole, Hispanics typically enjoy more default acceptance in more businesses and social groups (at least more than blacks do), but those businesses and groups in which open versions of this bias predominates are also less likely to modernize, and less likely to benefit from economic development than whiter or blacker areas as the years go by.

(The above aren't just San Antonio issues, by the way.)

- There is a heavy culture of advocacy for women, partly related to known issues with intimate partner violence and homicide. San Antonio is also a hub for human trafficking.

- San Antonio's sociocultural and economic divisions are easy to see if you have lived in the city long enough, with lines dividing the generally richer mixed and whiter North from the generally poorer Hispanic and blacker south; everyone knows what you mean when you refer to the "Westside," "Eastside," or "Kirby." It's just the way we've always known it, whether or not it has changed.

Many of these issues stem from the city's heavy emphasis on economic development at the expense of equal opportunity where—in line with the general culture—in-groups and businesses have more voice than citizens unless a social welfare program of some kind is involved. Social welfare or not, though, the class divisions are very real here, and delete from the lives of every class involved. (Consistent with mainstream San Antonio, I didn't even give our general Asian and Native American cultures a bullet, for example.) Only through the lens of business and the favored list of standard social lobbies does it seem easy for a constituency to get its foot in the door, so the city's responsiveness to the voices of its marginalized isn't nearly as strong as its response to the voices of those buying the up the land those marginalized live on.

Now I'll bet you think I'm claiming that San Antonio has race issues. It does. It may also sound like San Antonio's class and gender issues are strongly tied to its economic issues. They are. When a group or gender or political clique pools together and separates itself from others, it typically separates itself from much of what those others have to trade. We saw this in the discussion of communication among members of a microcollective. If incoming development is largely white and your region isn't conducive to that, your region won't enjoy the development. If your strong communities are heavily Hispanic and your region doesn't celebrate that, it won't enjoy the social favor. If your improvement zones and more affordable (but still quality) real estate comes with black areas and you don't have room for that, your market will more quickly get out of your control or stay unimproved. The areas of San Antonio, very broadly, reflect the economic consequences of sociocultural division. It's a taboo enough issue that you don't really hear about it without heavy pasteurization. Not surprisingly, you also don't hear many working fixes to economic segregation either.

That's not an accident. (Have you looked at a demographic map of Detroit?) Still, despite its divisions, you might be surprised that none of this makes San Antonio a "bad place" to be.

In my mind, San Antonio feels like a better place to be when it comes to addressing certain social issues. Its prejudices may exclude, but isn't nearly as destructive as other places I've lived, including among predominantly White, Korean, and Black populations. Its doors may be closed to you if you're not a business or don't fit the in-group mould, but you can almost always find a warm person somewhere among your circle to open that door anyway. If you've read my earlier books you know that I've gone back and forth on the city, but in general, karma comes around quickly here. The city carries a lot of human issues related to basic personal belonging, so it also has a lot of mechanisms for addressing those issues. Even as people from outside of San Antonio have begun to pour in in recent years—with more money and more education, taking the opportunities that native San Antonians have shown less qualified for overall—the city doggedly looks at its problem with as much honesty as it can. Its organizations continue to seek both social and economic solutions with all the data and action groups it can muster, with a recent shift more in the direction of equity after all.

But now why, despite plenty of efforts, has San Antonio been unable to fix its march towards lowered opportunity for its natives and political minorities as its market development skyrockets? I believe that the problem lies in the same factors that have influenced places like San Francisco and Detroit. When monetary capital is the sole measure of development, the rich will get richer and the poor will get poorer in all the ways you would expect. San Antonio is, however, amazingly rich in *social* capital—on the macro level of neighborhoods and the micro level of its clique cultures. As so many major American cities have not yet learned how to harness the value in their citizens' relationships to each other, these are still relegated to areas where you need to "know a guy" or have access to a shadow market. Some might think that turning a conversation about economy into a conversation about race is inappropriate, but it's not so much a race conversation as it is one of visible differences, how those visible differences can be easily converted into cultural separations and, hence, trade separations. But you need only look at international relations to see this kind of thing. Humans still love their heuristic boundaries, from the visible to the cultural, from the cultural to the sociopsychological. We won't play together emotionally, then wonder why the economic tallies don't add the way we want them to. I claim that San Antonio is one of the more honest places you'll find when it comes to even looking at cultural and identity issues in general.

The heavy economic development culture would convince you that you are poor because your land values are low, but doesn't count the extent to which you may have your needs almost fully met through your universe of relationships. Where other cities have failed, I honestly believe that San Antonio might be in a better position to remedy the disparities among its citizens simply because it is so relationship focused. In Los Angeles, the buses advertise movies. Here they advertise lawyers. People are actively looking for social solutions. The general city culture overall is more interested in staying the same in that relationship with its identity than it is in becoming different. In that sense, it may actually be closer to a solution that no similarly anti-melting pot, economically gold-rushed city to my knowledge has been able to obtain.

A Proposed Equity Solution

I spent a while dwelling on San Antonio in order to emphasize this point: So much of the city's economic direction is dictated by its social qualities, for better or worse. It also happens to be a very advocacy-focused city. It has to be. The private, keep-to-yourself bearing of New York or the open ambitiousness of L.A. isn't San Antonio's style. The culture does not favor group mixing nearly as much as it favors delineated identity. Still, *doing* things for groups that matter is very important here. Given all of the underlying social factors, we see in the city a kind of macro-psychological niche for ethnic pride which is as much a part of its personality as military and medical fields upon which it is partly built.

Our Objective

To decrease the divide between the haves and the apparent never-wills, we'll need to make use of the forms of social capital already inherent in the less money-affluent areas. The objective will be to provide monetary capital to these *social arrangements* rather than attempting to install a more traditional economic thinking into cultures that simply don't value this.

Even as an individual, you'll never get me to care as much about money as the President does. If you tried to train me through a business workshop, I might not be that interested. Instead, I have a culture that I care about. If you paid my culture or paid the results of my relationships with that culture, I might be interested all of a sudden. Entire geographic regions work the same way. You couldn't really pay the collective State of Texas that much for its diamonds. You could "pay" the collective State for its oil. The collective has a niche. Geographic regions in a city also have a niche. Furthermore, the idea of paying a group of people for their collective product has already been thoroughly tested. We call these jobs. If only a city found a way to pay its zip codes for what they produce, we might be able to employ sub-regions in the way we employ people. Civic microcollective funding holds this as its goal, and would work as follows:

Overview of Microcollective Funding (MCF)

Zip-Local Grant Applications

Where a city is unequal in the wealth of its sub-regions—by zip code for example—a grant-like process will allow a group of individuals exclusive to a zip code to apply for funding to carry out a specific enterprise in that zip code. Only individuals with business locations and pertinent interests exclusive to that zip code could apply for the funding, and this would hold for all zip codes associated with the city's annex—richer, poorer, or whatever. That is, every zip code would have a pool of money available to grant applicants located *only* in that region. If you had offices in two zip codes, you couldn't apply for any such funding anywhere under this program. The aim is to build up specific regions through the businesses or project groups exclusive to those regions.

The Money Comes From Two Places

The funds for a zip code's MCF come from a portion of taxes on vacant development as well as from a re-weighting of school-district taxes.

Vacant Property

When a person flips a house in a neighborhood where the homes are valued at $150,000 and sells it for $430,000, he could on the one hand, be accused of pricing out the people who live there. But now, what if we took the taxes which he is already paying on that overpriced house and diverted a considerable portion of it back into a pool of money designed to stay with that neighborhood? We don't want to punish the rich for simply doing their business, but we don't want to simply disenfranchise everyone else by driving up their taxes with no further improvements to their lives directly. Until a dwelling is filed as owner-occupied (and you'd need the required data system for seeing this), the property may be considered a value drain one way or another—until you divert its income generation back into the area where it sits AND allow the enterprises fit for that area to access such funds. Not just more construction crews repaving random streets in some other place. You price out my neighborhood? Part of your taxes come back to enterprises that my neighborhood specializes in forming. Some buyer may or may not take the house off your hands, and when they do, its role as a value drain will change, along with its taxation status.

Reweighted School Public School District Taxes

Consider that the role of a public school system is to educate the citizens of certain regions. Apportioning the fraction of each zip code that falls within a particular independent school district (ISD), we can now tie school districts to the MCF model. These will, in fact, be integral as we go on. Now even though the assumption is that ISDs educate children, we know full well that our ability to educate children depends largely on the cooperation of their parents. Also, their parents *were* children once.[5] What if ISDs also held, as part of their mission, the provision of services to the parents of their students as well? The adults who sustain the community in which the parents and children grow? The way we would arrange this requires several steps to work together if we are to avoid burdening the district. Here's how it would go:

- We begin by taking the ISD's existing tax revenue and reweighting it. 90% is allocated based on the usual provision of services while 10% of it is now allocated based on the effectiveness of its whole-district community programs.

- The ISD still gets 100% of its tax revenue, as long as its support services meet the standards of its city council district eligibility requirements (discussed shortly)

- The ISD, in order to administer the whole or partial zip codes assigned to it, has representatives which are part of an MCF

---

[5] That may sound naïve until you start thinking about what it means to be a K-12 educational provider, tied to P-16 + workforce outcomes.

oversight ("3+") committee. This is the group that actually awards and monitors the MCF grant projects currently running. In other words, the whole-district support services ARE the MCF projects—the whole portfolio of zip codes associated with that ISD.

- "Effectiveness" of a support service is determined at the city council level. It might be the case that one zip code needs to decrease the rates of domestic violence while another needs to raise workforce education as the goal for the current grant cycle, and that single ISD is the administrating region for both of these zips. In concert with the other members of its oversight committees, the ISD would award projects which addressed these issues, keeping each zip code's funding pool separate from those of other zip codes even within the same ISD. At the end of the cycle, a different set of evaluators on the city council level assesses whether the ISD's 3+ choices were actually effective. Here is where the entire city has a stake in a single ISD's and their constituent zip codes' provision of whole-local-community services and, in sum, whole-city beneficial services.

- Only if an ISD's oversight committee does a poor job in administering its awards, two years in a row, (with effectiveness determined by the city council district) does it run the risk of losing up to 10% of its tax revenue for the next year.

Where does that 10% go?

It still goes to the zip codes who need it, but is *administered* by a different advisory board, this time possibly including representatives from private (instead of the main public) educational entities in the same district. The other entities do *not* get to keep that money. The ISD essentially loses it for that year, and instead of it going to the them as it normally would, that money joins the vacant property money for distribution among the MCF awardees. Had this not happened, the MCF money would have only consisted of the vacant tax money. The ISD would have gotten the full amount, but would have been expected to make some of its resources available to the awardees for the sake of meeting the city council global goals. When the ISD fails to award or administer properly two years in a row, that 10% becomes real money proportionally added to the MCF pool for each zip code, and the award is administered by a different group.

- The ISD can petition to get its 10% back the next year given an improvement plan for how its advisory boards will chose awardees. There will be a 1 year probation period in this case.

Program Oversight

If I currently run a school district, I already have my hands full. It may seem like MCF proposes to threaten 10% of my funding if I don't take care of this new thing. That's partly true, but the ISD doesn't administer the grants alone. Instead, administration of MCF awards is conducted by representatives from the ISD, industry, and higher education: a "3+" committee. The 3+ committee reviews the grant applications, awards, and monitors the recipient programs to ensure that they do indeed meet the zip-local goals for the current grant cycle. As a reminder, only zip-local applicants are eligible to apply for the MCF awards, their projects must benefit the region in question, and the 3+ committees themselves are subject to evaluation at the city council level. When a person in a particular zip code has a project which he or she believes will benefit that area, they can combine with other people to enact it. Priority is largely determined by the 3+ as function of each region's specific needs, though it doesn't have to matter whether the project is a business, a class, an event, or anything else. Any type of endeavor (including not-so-monetary microcollectives from two chapters ago) are eligible to be funded, as long as the projects can be accomplished in a fairly short time (within the year of award).

Ethical Protections

The are some features of MCF which are designed to protect the original goals of the program.

- A group can be awarded an MCF grant up to three times, after which they will need to seek funding from elsewhere. That may not please some people, but the goal is to promote agility and mobility in a zip code, not another cushy business which ties up opportunities for new entrants.

- If a 3+ committee fails to meet city council evaluations standards, it is possible that the replacement advisory group can just be the 3+ group from another ISD. However,

- the funds allocated to a particular zip code never leave that zip code. Even if its administering 3+ group is unfit, even if

there are no eligible applicants in a
particular year and the money just sits
there. This is a protection against the kind
of convenient disinvestment that drives
economic segregation in the first place.
Regardless of what happens, a region's
MCF pool—its portion of the vacant
property taxes along with any failed ISD-
cycle money—<u>never</u> leaves that region.

- If there are no qualified applicants in a
  year, the 3+ group will report this to the
  city council (so that people know the ISD
  isn't just dodging its duties in
  administering that 10%); such reports have
  to be provided separately for every zip code
  which produced no awardees. A district
  with five zip codes under its charge and
  only one award may be suspect, and the
  city council has the right to cite the 3+
  group as failing standard for that year
  simply because it didn't try hard enough to
  address the MCF regional goals by letting
  the public know that the program existed.
  We're trying to empower the most local-
  level regions we can through this program.
  It is not cool for an ISD to thwart this goal
  through silent self-interest—failing to
  award just because it doesn't want to put
  its 10% on the line. For the public

education provider one way or another, the 10% is ALWAYS on the line.

- If there are no qualified applicants in a year, the city holds the money in accounting until the next cycle. The ISD and advisory board will then have to petition the city to release that money if they want to include it in the next year's allocations. This is to protect against advisory boards suddenly squandering a multi-year pile up of unallocated funds on one year of bad awards. There are limits on how much of a piled up pot you can dip into.

- The MCF is available to every district, every zip code. Even the very richest region should have a fund available. What we hope to have here is socioeconomic improvement in problem zips, forward social innovation in already high performing regions. Let it not be said, though, that MCF was another welfare program targeted only towards the poor. If we want true social equity, we need truly equal opportunity. Again, it doesn't make sense to punish the rich when it's their resources driving much of your economic progress. Everyone has access to an MCF for their region, to address the issues which the citizens who live there know best.

Recap

Microcollective funding, or MCF, is a proposed mechanism for combating the kinds of inequity that describe places like San Antonio and San Francisco. Cities like San Antonio, which are more systematically seeking solutions to the problems of unequal opportunity on the citizen level may be in a better position to introduce a program like MCF for granting monetary value to social capital-type enterprises which directly benefit a whole region. In order to connect primary education, secondary education, and the workforce expertise towards the growth of a local area that would otherwise have been left behind or capitalistically exploited, MCF is administered by "3+" groups which look to award small group endeavors of almost any kind which can make their mark in a year, in line with the issues known to exist in that particular area.

Public school districts, to the extent that they are the first-line trainers of tomorrow's citizens, may also reach back to the people who are already past graduating age. They do this by assigning their seats on 3+ committees which distribute primarily vacant-property tax revenue the qualified applicants. Since we're working with tiny groups, even an award as small as a few hundred dollars might pay for a highly successful community event, so the money available need not be a giant sum. If however a 3+ group fails to administer its MCF charges properly, up to 10% of the associated ISD's regular tax revenue may be in jeopardy. The best thing an ISD's 3+ group can do is award wisely and monitor responsibly. This doesn't mean that the ISD will actually need to spend any of that 10% on an MCF programs. It is expected, however, that the ISD will contribute any reasonable resources or facilities access to help its awardees succeed. The district will essentially be choosing private citizens to help it carry out its broader social mission beyond that of a static education provider.

How does MCF address inequity issues like economic segregation? It assumes that, where a subregion lacks the socioeconomic opportunities of its neighbors, the people in that region must still be making a living somehow—presumably via an excess of undervalued *social* capital. MCF allows applicants in a region to get paid for pooling the social and psychological capital they are used to, given that these are also applied to issues which the city level cares about. Furthermore, since comingling is not allowed across regions, no matter how mismanaged or faultily administered a regional award may be, the MCF funding that comes from a region stays in that region, with additional protections against awardees receiving funding more than three times, replacement committees disinvesting in the native community, and 3+ groups not awarding at all. The aim is to finally reward what a region is good at.

Clearly the MCF awards that originate in one region can benefit everyone everywhere. Only the sourced funds are confined to that region. In this chapter's example I used zip codes, but realistically we would use census tracts, subdivisions, separate municipalities, and other more statistically homogenous groupings to establish our MCF regions. The ISDs would still be the chief vehicle for the program, but in cities with only one ISD or a different kind of public education structure, we would divide as is fitting for the city.

One last note on implementing microcollective funding: Suppose I'm a city in fiscal danger, and I need all the money I can get. MCF appears to rob me of a certain amount of property tax revenue while doling it back out to citizens who may not actually give a damn. There are two answers to this.

1. A small group of people is not a city. A $2,000 trial award for an MCF program shouldn't kill anyone. If it does, the city has bigger management issues that could just as easily be solved through staffing decision. But even a flat $1000 per sub-region trial of MCF program opens the civic governing body to an entire space of potential solutions which its own staff of ISDs wouldn't otherwise be in a position to handle. It needs to be open to the whole city however, as a less consistent array of spotted "promise zones" or development zones have—as I've seen in San Antonio—fostered more opportunistic emigration of private businesses, pricing out, gentrification, and further inequity than they have genuine social solutions. A trial won't kill a city, but if not everyone has access to the same opportunity regardless of subregion or socioeconomic tier, self-interest will drive who participates from the very beginning.

2. If your city manager is really reluctant to divert existing vacant property taxes, they can always experiment with diverting taxes

above a threshold. So the MCF money pool would only be built from taxes on newer development, flips beyond those that currently exist, or incoming groups resulting from certain community incentives. It doesn't have to be all or nothing. It might not even be built from vacant property at all. The city may build up its MCF pool from any type of reasonably capitalizable object which represents a problematic drain on the regions in which it is located. Just don't raise taxes. We're fixing inefficiencies, not creating new ones. We want people to be excited about the possibilities for civic remedies, not angry that they're being imposed on *again*.

The overall idea is, even if you are a city in dire straits, you still have sections of your city which continue to apply certain non-capital resources despite you. If you're not interested in rewarding those social or psychological (niche talent) markets through some kind of monetarily useful program, those resources can just be expected to sit there. But if you have a system for turning untapped non-capital into capital resources—starting just by setting up some experimental committees, you may also have a system for turning around the direction your city has been taking.

As long as monetary capital remains the great measure of a city's progress, that city will, not surprisingly, measure its worth by it. Yet in order for a governmental administrative unit to function, it—like a person—must obtain its monetary capital by trading out its psychological and social capital, while fostering a certain level of cultural and domestic security among its people (emotional capital). If we don't make plans to tap into these non-monetary elements in addressing our economic divisions, the non-monetary elements will instead operate anyway in the form of the shadow market, social problems, and unmet psychological talent needs. To put those non-monetary forms of capital to use represents a step in the direction of a full-value economic system of the kind that many people have long been able to build on a personal level as they more intentionally direct their efforts towards the endeavors most worthwhile.

References

About the starred references

Much of this chapter reflects my own personal experience, and like all personal experiences that anyone might have had, is limited to one person and doesn't require a citation. I have, however, included some sources below which can give you more context for the kinds of situations I have described. Just because the sources are there, however, doesn't mean that what I've said applies to everyone's perspective. Obviously. The issues I've described in this chapter, though, are real enough to warrant both discussion and further attempts at solutions, so I *have* raised them. And although it might at first seem inappropriate to introduce so many social issues into the discussion of capital, the importance of monetary capital *is* heavily socialized, where the writing of this book actually began with my own attempts to understand the various barriers to mobility in my own city. As I mentioned in *Laurentia*, it doesn't make sense, to me, to divorce a topic from the problem it was meant to solve.

At the time of this writing, we live in a society where the natural reaction is to become angry with something just because an issue is raised, from statues being pulled down to legal cases with celebrities. From there, the solution is often creation of further lines between the rich and the working, the black and the blue, the liberal and the conservative. That's unfortunate. Whether it's a president attempting to work with the other party or a researcher studying the perpetrators of violence, our society—despite the freedom of speech—is just a skittish place. Accordingly, real dialogues are frequently difficult to have as the parties feel lost without their entrenchments. My views of San Antonio and the culture here in particular are bound to be misread by someone looking for a fight, despite everything else I've said about these things. I could tell you "That's not what I was saying" a million times, but at some point, if someone isn't listening, they just aren't listening. It would be a waste to explain gray perspectives to people who only see black and white. Until that conversational terrain changes however, the people who say they're about equality but won't meet at the table with their opposition, without defensiveness, without the combat stance, might just be blowing wind.

why this is 207

Stoeltje, M. F. (2017). Worlds apart: Concentrated poverty and an increasing income divide make San Antonio one of the country's most segregated cities. Retrieved January 6, 2020 from http://projects. expressnews.com/stoeltje-worlds-apart-poverty-income-inequality-bexar#chapter-1829740

and will be for years to come 207

World Population Review (2019). San Antonio. Retrieved   January   6,   2020   from http://worldpopulationreview.com/us-cities/san-antonio-population/

*for reasons that must have existed 208

Goldberg, R. A. (1983). Racial change of the Southern periphery: The case of San Antonio, Texas, 1960–1965. *Journal of Southern History, 49*(3), 349. Retrieved January 6, 2020 from https://search. ebscohost.com/login.aspx?direct=true&db =25h&AN=33852076&site=ehost-live

*As do Mexicans...under the current... 208

Delgado, D. J. (2016). 'And You Need Me to Be the Token Mexican?': Examining racial hierarchies and the complexities of racial identities for middle class Mexican Americans. *Critical Sociology, 42*(4/5), 679–698.

*where whites divide...become more obvious. 209

Walsh, C. (2011). Erasing race, dismissing class: San Antonio Independent School District V. Rodriguez. *Berkeley La Raza Law Journal, 21*, 133–171.

*Hispanics typically enjoy more... 210

Abrica, E. J., García-Louis, C., & Gallaway, C. D. J. (2020). Antiblackness in the Hispanic-serving community college (HSCC) context: Black male collegiate experiences through the lens of settler colonial logics. *Race, Ethnicity & Education, 23*(1), 55–73.

The above aren't just San Antonio issues 210

Huang, Y., South, S. J., Spring, A., & Crowder, K. (2018). A decomposition of trends in blacks' and whites' exposure to other-race neighbors, 2001–2011. *City & Community, 17*(3), 590–614.

*culture of advocacy for women, partly... 210

Stoeltje, M. F. (2019). As family violence fatalities in San Antonio increase, women's advocates take to the streets. Retrieved January 6, 2020 from https://www.expressnews.com/news/local/article/As-family-violence-fatalities-in-San-Antonio-13751706.php

is also a hub for human trafficking 211

Norris, N. (2019). BCSO: San Antonio is a hotbed for human trafficking. Retrieved January 6, 2020 from https://news4sanantonio.com/news/local/bcso-sa-is-a-hotbed-for-human-trafficking

*easy to see 211

Statistical Atlas (2020). Race and ethnicity in San Antonio, Texas. Retrieved January 6, 2020 from https://statisticalatlas.com/place/Texas/San-Antonio/Race-and-Ethnicity

*emphasis on economic...at the expense of... 211

Jefferson, G. (2019). A stronger economic foundation for San Antonio. Retrieved January 6, 2020 from https://www.expressnews.com/business/business_columnists/greg_jefferson/article/A-stronger-economic-foundation-for-San-Antonio-14583366.php

*that San Antonio has race issues. It does 212

National League of Cities. (2018). City profile on racial equity: San Antonio, Texas.

strongly tied to its economic issues. They are 212

Hill, T. D., Burdette, A. M., Jokinen, G. H. M., & Brailsford, J. M. (2013). Neighborhood disorder, social support, and self-esteem:

Evidence from a sample of low-income women living in three cities. *City & Community, 12*(4), 380–395.

*It's a taboo enough issue 212

Craig, H. K., & Lewis, R. (2015). Methodological considerations and challenges to conducting research on interethnic relationships: Using the right toolkit! *Journal of Social Issues, 71*(4), 675–692.

with more money and more education 213

Jefferson, G. (2019). Poverty, poor schools go hand in hand. Retrieved January 6, 2020 from https://www.expressnews.com/business/business_columnists/greg_jefferson/article/Poverty-poor-schools-go-hand-in-hand-14487451.php

*the city doggedly looks at its problem... 213

City of San Antonio (2020). Office of Equity overview. Retrieved January 6, 2020 from https://www.sanantonio.gov/Equity/About

*have not yet learned how to harness... 214

Katz, T., & Barol, J. (2017). Building a village: Tapping into untapped resources. *Journal of Vocational Rehabilitation, 46*(3), 301–303.

a conversation about economy into...race 214

Killewald, A., & Bryan, B. (2018). Falling behind: The role of inter- and intragenerational processes in widening racial and ethnic wealth gaps through early and middle adulthood. *Social Forces, 97*(2), 705–740.

need only look at international relations 214

Kaya, A. (2020). Right-wing populism and Islamophobism in Europe and their impact on Turkey–EU relations. *Turkish Studies, 21*(1), 1–28.

their heuristic boundaries 215

Kahneman, D. (2011). T*hinking, fast and slow*. New York: Farrar, Straus and Giroux.

Krosch, A. R., & Amodio, D. M. (2014). Economic scarcity alters the perception of race. *Proceedings of the National Academy of Sciences, 111*(25), 9079-9084.

*might be in a better...so relationship focused 215

Ferilli, G., Sacco, P. L., Tavano Blessi, G., & Forbici, S. (2017). Power to the people: When culture works as a social catalyst in urban regeneration processes (and when it does not). *European Planning Studies, 25*(2), 241–258.

for pooling the social and psychological... 228

Palmer, L., & Bhargava, V. (2018). Forms of wealth associated with attaining peer group net worth following bankruptcy. *Social Science Quarterly, 99*(1), 97–117.

self-interest will drive who participates 230

García-Viñuela, E. (2019). Income-preserving political finance reforms: Evidence from three Spanish reforms. *Revista Española de Investigaciones Sociologicas, 167*, 3–18.

If you're not...monetarily useful program 231

Liscow, Z. (2018). Is efficiency biased? *University of Chicago Law Review, 85*(7), 1649–1718.

by trading out its psychological and social... 232

Duranton, G. & Puga, D. (2019). Urban growth and its aggregate implications. *NBER Working Paper Series 26591*.

Chapter 13: Conclusion

When we speak of non-capital wealth, we're referring primarily to capital of the monetary kind. But even non-monetary resources can be converted to capital. Our everyday markets attempt to do this all the time. There is, however, a fundamental paradox that comes with near-universal commodification: where we aim to assign value to things which defy the normal countable bounds, we will always be faced with the boundary-defiant aspects of our bounded system. The more we attempt to measure with money, the more real those things which are not measurable by money will become. Thus the basic *innovation which replaces one piece of technology with another, *social issues, *disposition rights related to our possessions, and the more relational *terms of trade which govern our buying and selling in the first place all become increasingly resistant to having an agreed upon value assigned to them. It means less and less in the long run to say that "This TV is worth $1000 but that other TV from one decade earlier was 'worth' $1500." Our

242

circumstances, our standards of experience, and our relations with the rest of the world all add or take away capital value despite defying measure. In this book we have explored a system for integrating three other dimensions into our capital picture, further investigating their nature and how to build them.

In a world rich in tradable, publicly agreed upon value, there are still many subjective things we will never agree on and many worthwhile things whose value will remain impossibly abstract. For these combinations of normative agreement and abstraction versus tangibility, we have a total of four kinds of capital. One of the primary roles of markets is to trade two at a time—one capital form for another.

Monetary capital has brought us a long way as a society, as people who would never otherwise agree consistently on the value of items or acts find an efficient way to bypass complex negotiations and get on with the trade itself. But now that there are so many opportunities to trade—so many ways for people to acquire their desires even without the value to back it, so many ways for things that aren't real (like opportunity, risk, and convenience) to command some of the highest returns available—we now find ourselves in an age where we don't need nearly as much to ask whether we *can* obtain an expensive product, loan, or line of credit. Rather, we're pressed even harder to ask if we *should*. When the monetary capital we receive will ultimately go towards psychological, emotional, or relational ends (with health and security being a combination of these), we're ultimately challenged to prioritize whether pursuit of money as a middle man before these is worth it. The mechanisms for making money are well tested. For some people the routes are very easy. For others those same routes are very hard. But once you have it, what then? The routes to role efficacy, relationship quality, and emotional fulfillment are also well tested. They too can be measured, but their quality attainment isn't always related to your money.

Four Kinds of Capital

In order to build complete lives in the age of data and measure, we take on the challenge of adding non-monetary capital wealth to our list of priorities, converting it into a family of familiar yet often undervalued forms.

- **Money** – measures in public thresholds, and trades in objects between owner and receiver; it goes from $0...\infty$. You can use it when you and the other party can agree on the basic form *and* the basic value of the traded thing.

Money owed might be considered negative, but your debts aren't paid in negative money from you. They're paid in positive money from somebody else. So there isn't really such a thing as negative money outside the convenient theoretical world of accounting. Conceptually negative money is actually positive money obligated in the opposite direction of the counter.

- **Role Efficacy** – is measured as a private optimum and displayed as actions from an owner to a receiving party; it goes from 0...100%. This is what you build when you can agree on the form *but not* the value of a traded thing.

  If only you could put out an ad saying, "Now Hiring Great Leaders," and be done with it. But that ad won't work. You'd do better to let your leading culture speak to those potential leaders for you.

- **Fulfillment** – is measured on a private threshold and trades in "desire states" *within* the owner; it ranges from $-\infty...0...\infty$, and is used where you *can't agree on the form or the value* of the traded thing.

Maybe it isn't the price tag. Maybe it isn't even an "it." It might be a "how" or a "why." Some people can only be recruited to your cause based on your paths to an end rather than the measurable end itself. So your how and why stopped lining up with that other person? No wonder the payment stopped being enough. You tried to buy their journey one floor board at a time.

When it comes to fulfillment, you can be a source or super-supplier $(+\infty)$, as well as a sink or vacuum $(-\infty)$ on top of being a basic supplier $(+1)$ or demander (-1).

- **Relationships** – are measured against a public optimum of "familiarity," displayed as an extent of actions passable from owner to receiver; they go from $-1... 0...1$. Here you *can't agree on the form, but can agree on the value* of what you're trading.

So there's this thing you'd like to have happen. You'll know exactly how to measure it when it happens, but the way it actually gets done is more of a mystery to you. Sounds like you need the foggy inner workings of another party to take care of it for you. Don't count too much on buying those inner workings.

You can see yourself as knowing (towards) another (+1) as well as being known by another (-1), with grades of familiarity in between.

Notice how, even if we wanted to, we couldn't measure the three other forms of capital in terms of money. The notion of scarcity alone means that money will never be a complete measure of things like role efficacy or fulfillment, which are effectively infinite or infinitely perfectable in the world of the owner. Relationships aren't infinite, but the kinds of things sharable within them include fulfillment and role efficacy.

Microcollectives

Once we understand all of the possible forms of wealth available to us, we can then identify the ones we're best at handling. Perhaps surprisingly, we found two: our psychological niche and, later, a hint at the existence of its traded partner, whatever that was. This was discussed in the chapters on valuation micromarkets. One of the highest uses of your niche is to trade it to others who need it in exchange for something which you yourself are a vacuum for.

Because psychology-specific needs will vary everywhere you go, we found that establishing a market for your unique product pair can produce great rewards. So if you are a great social connector and as well as an automatic vacuum for emotional support, you might create a micromarket with someone else who is either a vacuum for social connections or a great source of emotional support. You would then expand your micromarket to include yet another person who trades in whatever the first person couldn't trade with you. This will hold for everyone in your designed market, and the result is something that looks like a business, runs like a creative team, and may or may not care about money. Unlike a traditional business, this group which you form is aimed at the highest fulfilling expression of the people in it, not necessarily the results of those people's labor. Your micromarket will evolve a vacuum of its own as well as a role effective niche of its own, beyond that of your individual group members, yet reflective of your sum. If you can hold your group together through the various challenges that visit it, you'll find it to be one of the most personally rewarding endeavors you've ever undertaken, even if it didn't meet the classic pressure to make money and even if you never figure out what motivates your fellow market mates to value things in the foreign ways that they do.

Socioeconomic tiers

It turns out that monetary capital is okay. Yet so many monetarily rich people are neither wealthy nor happy, as they may be missing the psychological or emotional fulfillment assumed to come with their level of money. Their relationships may even be of lower quality to the extent that it is the socioeconomic status and not like-mindedness that ties them to those relationships. As on all tiers Poor through Ultra Rich, this skewing of ends may even apply within their closest partnerships.

Although it was fairly unscientific, I shared some observations I've made over the years traversing different social tiers. The most surprising find to me was that the Lower Middle Class seem to be genuinely happier with themselves than most other tiers—not because they were lazy without a care, but actually for the opposite reason. Within their spheres of influence, they feel (and often are) more *role* efficacious and more socially cooperative than their richer or poorer society-mates. The second most surprising finding in my mind is how, when you consider monetary capital to constitute only one piece of a larger puzzle, the second-highest tier Rich have the most collective power and some of the least individual social sphere-effectiveness of all. Power over employees, service providers and certain peers, yes. Empowerment to make the worlds they live in respond to their truly highest personal wishes, not so much. On the level of entire classes, the Ultra Rich and Lower Middle seem to have more of such empowerment than anyone else. Where do you land in these tiers? Not just monetarily, but across *all* forms of capital?

(As I'm writing this book, my own social tier has moved away from Middle Class closer towards Lower Upper Class. My challenge to people on both the Lower Upper and Rich tiers is to do something significant—in line with our psychological niches, but outside of the purchasable lifestyle packages—which would continue to fulfill us AND fulfill the kinds of emotional worlds we build, even if all the money and its objects went away.)

Microcollective Funding

Given that our different socioeconomic tiers all share the same geographic spaces, we ended with a proposal for channeling non-monetary capital towards more globally equitable ends. Microcollective funding (MCF) took one typical drain on a local area—vacant property—and used it to fund innovative, objective driven microcollectives specific to that area. Public school districts, ISDs, were the chief vehicles for administering this program because such an assignment was considered to be an extension of their roles as publicly supported education providers. Yet the ISDs weren't expected to shoulder this wider social effort alone. Instead, they held seats on a system of formal "3+" advisory boards which also included representatives from industry and higher education. Together these boards determined what did and didn't make for a qualified project, and ensured that the ISD's regional portion of the city's whole MCF was properly overseen. To compel such active, quality oversight, the 3+ groups were to be evaluated yearly at city council, with failed boards resulting in a potential loss of up to 10% of the ISD revenue.

The 10% penalty, by the way, is not the only monetary outcome for an ISD. There is a positive one. If I am an ISD tasked with administering 10 regions of MCF (prohibited from mixing their funds with each other), I essentially have a say in how 10 regions' worth of vacant tax allocation gets spent—probably in my favor. Obviously there would be the required disclosures of relationship and conflict of interest, but basically, I could pessimistically see MCF as threatening to turn my tax-derived $1 into $0.90 if I fail, or I could see it as turning my $1 into $1.07 with the $0.07 allocated to awardees doing projects which will ultimately benefit my district. Yes there is the burden of overseeing the MCFs, but in exchange for overseeing these, I also enjoy a yearly applicant pool of private citizens inventing all kinds of solutions for solving issues not otherwise under my purview. Parental involvement, poverty, crime, environmental threats... I may yet need these to be addressed in order for the issues facing my schools to really get solved, but I can't tackle these as a school district. My MCF awardees can.

Final Thoughts

I grew up somewhere in the Middle Class and have been there for most of my life. Only now is that changing. As our society tends to train us, some might say that an economic idea not sponsored by a millionaire is not worth listening to. But it depends on what aspects of economy you're looking at. Happy people are good sources of happiness. Connected people are good sources of connections. And fulfilled people tend to be good sources of fulfillment. For you too I'd say that your worth doesn't need to be circumscribed by the money-only parts of the American Dream and its outward symbols. Even if you have attained that dream already, your worth doesn't have to be fully determined by it. If there is something within you which you know is great, which you've long wanted to trade with the world, that may be the thing which most of your other forms of riches are forever aimed at accessing. Think about finding some trading partners in that thing. Consider receiving trades in what they have to give. If more people did this I believe our world would be a lot less frustrated in the lives it thinks status should buy. Perspective is what we need.

As always, I've enjoyed the exploration with you. Go trade your best with someone and receive their best in return.